A DEFINING PATHS AUTHOR SERIES

Love the Skin YOU'RE In

How to Conquer Life Through Divergent Thinking

DR. VIRGINIA LeBLANC

Author: Dr. Virginia LeBlanc
Title: Love the Skin YOU'RE In
ISBN (Softcover): 978-0-9990532-0-1
     (Hardcover): 978-0-9990532-1-8
Category: SELF-HELP/Motivational & Inspirational

Defining Paths Author Series
Defining Paths
3430 Connecticut Ave. NW
Washington, DC 20008

....

Printed in the United States of America

A DEFINING PATHS AUTHOR SERIES

Love the Skin YOU'RE In

How to Conquer Life Through Divergent Thinking

DR. VIRGINIA LeBLANC

Written for such a time as this.

Dedicated to my magnificent god-daughter,

Savannah Johnson Phillips.

You are everything you need to be.

You are more than a conqueror.

Keep doing you!

With love,
Auntie Gi

LOVE THE *Skin* YOU'RE IN

Table Of Contents

LOVE THE *Skin* YOU'RE IN

Preface

Before we begin, thank you sincerely for picking up my book. Now that pleasantry is out of the way, let's talk about reality and the real of life . . .

Have you traveled through life feeling that you are different, not quite comfortable in your skin, like you don't belong or are even an outsider trying to fit in? Do you feel trapped or suffocated by social norms and expectations, judged by those who suggest you are not hitting the mark when you know in your spirit that mark is not for you? If you relate to these questions, this book is for you. The timeless message of *Love the Skin YOU'RE In* is not meant for any one gender, race, ethnicity, class, or age group but for all who feel drawn according to their life story and where they might be on their journey.

This is not a scholarly dissertation. Please do not expect one. I am not your "normal" scholar, inasmuch as you will find the "Dr." hat mostly off as you take this journey with me. However, you will find it from time to time throughout these pages. When called for, I dress it up, and when not, I dress it down, whatever is required as life has taught me this invaluable skill. I want to meet you where you are and lift you up. *Love the Skin YOU'RE In* will lend insight into how I learned and went about this and other life lessons in the loss, suppression, and re-emergence of my individuality. It is meant to open eyes, inspire, and empower you to transform your life. It is not meant to tell you how to live your life but rather to give suggestions on how to go about it based on my experience, if you wish to restore your individuality and to conquer life. I share what I know to be true in my reality and the facts about life I have discovered. This book was not developed out of a denunciation of society but rather from a real and intentioned place for your heart health and holistic well-being. It has been brewing for at least ten years, but the message came clear in September 2016 along with clarity of my purpose to move people and entities to action by breaking their chains and helping to change their present and future reality for the better.

Throughout life I have not only learned how to connect the dots through divergent thinking but also gained permission and freedom to be who I am and was meant to be. I have always had a mind that leaned toward empowerment. This calling was rediscovered during my time in Bloomington, Indiana, as director of the Hudson and Holland Scholars Program at Indiana University. More than any other place and time, Bloomington taught me essential life lessons when life happens . . . Watershed moments make, break, and/or redefine you in changing your course. These moments, these experiences, are pivotal and eye opening if you see them for what they are—teaching moments in rediscovering the true you. You will discover that fear is power and that it has no power over you that you do not give it. There's no magic bullet, no quick fix. What is important at one point in your life will be different at another point. Accept it, embrace it, and keep moving forward.

Love the Skin YOU'RE In: How to Conquer Life through Divergent Thinking is written out of my love for humanity and desire to encourage and empower all those seeking their place and desiring to fulfill their purpose in life. If you want to take a journey in unconventional, unsocialized wisdom and experience, you will want to keep reading this book for practical guidance on how to get and put it together for a sustainable win. I share REAL lessons learned and "how-tos" throughout. I have had to learn to love the skin I'm in in a number of ways, literally and figuratively, in an ethnic, gender, cultural, physical, spiritual, and mentally conscious way. In the process, I discovered that perspective is everything and that it comes from mind-set and experience. There is no one way to do things; therefore, there is no right or wrong way to live life so long as you are accountable and accept responsibility for your choices. Love, pain, shame, loss, grief, and all potential emotions are a part of the journey ... I get it now ... For so long, I didn't and tried to shut it all out, which was cheating and stunting my growth. I just didn't know how to handle it other than the way I was socially conditioned to handle it. For me, that was burying it all. Yet in choosing this option, you put up walls and shut out everything that makes you who you are and could be. You falsely believe nothing affects you, nothing matters, but things do matter. Things happen that can't be undone. What then? Too many of us walk in denial and for far too long, if we ever emerge from denial at all. It requires changing your mind-set and way of being, both of which are difficult to do because you may be unfamiliar with how to go about this. Change is hard, but we need to engage in more of it. Once you take that first step, then the second, and ultimately the third, the taste is undeniable. It's a taste of capability, freedom, empowerment, and transformation unlike anything you've tasted before. You will want more for yourself and others, hence, my decision to write and to share my knowledge with you.

My journey and twenty plus years of experience across the globe living a colorful, divergent life as an author, speaker, singer, coach, consultant, educator, and executive (to name a few) have produced a wealth of knowledge and a portfolio of competencies that make me an expert, authority, or guru (whatever your preference) uniquely qualified to write on this subject. I have been fortunate to live many different lives all in one, preparing me for any obstacle or challenge in life. It's all about setting your mind right and conquering your fear of life and potential outcomes. Once you do that, and realize that you are truly in the driver's seat, you become more powerful than you could ever imagine. Then, you are ready to achieve what you believe. *Love the Skin YOU'RE In* debunks societal notions that we must travel identified paths or follow a formula to conquer life and find success. It asserts the individual, qualitative nature of success, as opposed to quantifiable measures. What is "success" for one is not success for another. Life is about walking your path, connecting the dots, and finding purpose and fulfillment because you have been led by your heart and the truth of who you are—strong, intelligent, diverse, adaptable, wise, and tried by fire. You were meant to do and be more. You were meant to be different!

Walk with me, talk with me, respectfully disagree with me, but do something. Gain new perspective, validation, and permission to believe in yourself, walk your path, set personal measures and move forward to achieve your measure of success. If you are enticed even a little bit, keep reading . . .

Acknowledgments

To *my Lord and Savior, Jesus Christ,* my rock and the author and finisher of my faith – He has carried, covered, and strengthened me through it all. The manifestation of this book and its message to love yourself and humanity from the inside out has been under His inspiration and guidance. Through Him, I have found my purpose!

To *my mother, Flo LeBlanc-Stovall* – What to say about my extraordinary mother and earthly angel, Flo? You put the "extra" in ordinary. I have watched your life journey with sheer amazement. I have always said, if I can be half the woman you are—strong, intelligent, caring, committed, loving, selfless, confident, and comfortable in the skin you're in—I would be good, and I feel pretty great. I love, respect, and appreciate you more than you can ever know. Thank you for your sacrifices, guidance, and unconditional love. Mom, no matter end results, you chose well. I am who I am because of it. THANK YOU!!!

To *my brother, Brandon LeBlanc* – I love the skin I'm in even more because of your presence in my life; I couldn't have asked for a more perfect gift. Thank you for your unconditional love and support! Appreciate you always having my back.

Finally, thank you to *ALL* loved ones, colleagues, and acquaintances who have been a part of my life in whatever way. You have been my unexpected muse in life and motivation in writing this book. I am because you are/were (RIP, Granny, Grammie, Papa and Daddy).

Introduction

Life can throw serious punches. The pressure to conform to societal norms and expectations is enormous and drilled into us. Rarely are divergent tendencies in thinking encouraged and our uniqueness too easily relegated to a back burner for the sake of societal constructs. How do you get up and keep going when life knocks you down? You get back up with new perspective and divergent thinking, two of your most important assets, "cornermen" in the boxing ring of life. Your reality may appear bleak, but perspective is everything; you do not have to conform. When feeling weak, find your way to the corner. When abandoned, find your way to the corner. When bullied, find your way to the corner. When being attacked mentally, physically, or spiritually, find your way to the corner. When just feeling "some kind of way," find your way to the corner. Perspective sheds light amid darkness and lends power to the powerless. In combination with divergent thinking, it will help you gather your thoughts, see you through any situation, and teach you that no one and nothing has power over you but you. You have the gift of choice, and it's up to you what you do with it.

Love the Skin YOU'RE In is my love letter to society based on my personal experience on how to overcome and conquer life through divergent thinking. So, what is divergent thinking? You will have to read chapter 5, "Divergent Thinking: Thinking without a Box," for greater insight. Suffice it to say that it is a foundational means that you should not live without in not only everyday life but also in extraordinary circumstances. Divergent thinking will set you apart, give you the advantage, and help you connect the dots for solutions in pursuit of YOUR definition of success. That definition will change along the way, so do not be afraid to allow the transformation process to occur. Those of you who are divergent souls are hardwired to keep going no matter what. If you are not divergent by nature, you must tap into your willpower to find your strength. The ability to redefine yourself is yet another gift. Don't fear it and don't hide from it. The person you discover along that changing path will either reaffirm, confirm, or surprise you.

Social paradigms and conditioning can cause us to lose or suppress individuality. *Love the Skin YOU'RE In* opens eyes to renaissance and discovery of that individuality. It carries both a literal and figurative connotation. Sadly, most of us walk around in what we believe to be our true self, when in fact it is not. We have not gone through experiences, processes, or regular self-assessments that might allow us to uncover the root causes of our behavior and heal from our hurts, hangs-ups, and habits in life (Thank you, Celebrate Recovery!). We walk around with blinders on, coping as best we've learned how, and repeat in our mind's eye that we are okay when we are not; repeat anything to yourself enough times, and you will eventually believe it. However, understanding key elements in your discovery process and how they apply, aside from the usual 1-2-3 construct so common in societal structures, can make all the difference. While in theory there isn't anything wrong with using a linear method; a great number of my colleagues use them. The detriment in doing so, however, is that the human mind wants to take the easy route. It wants to be conditioned, and these methods provide an easy solution. "Easy" does not get you ahead. It merely facilitates the norm. Every person's journey is different, and you should allow for that difference to manifest and take form in the ring of life. If you do not, life will eventually knock you out for the victory.

You have the potential to be and live extraordinarily. You simply need insight into how to find and keep the advantage and it starts with self-love. At some point, life forces us all to put on masks for protection. The important thing is to recognize and rectify that fact by taking it off. *Love the Skin YOU'RE In* frees you from thoughts of abnormality versus normality and validates your individuality. You are your own benchmark (no one else). While life will undoubtedly throw everything at you when seeking your place in it; it is all a part of the experience. A pervading theme throughout this book is to learn to love even amid pain, disappointment, adversity, and difference and life will reward you with the greatest possibilities. Love, or a lack thereof, bends the rules for or against you. Finding that fine line between fear and strength in this pursuit is not so easy, just as things are not so black and white as we would like to think. There are shades in everything. You must find the right shades for you along life's journey to reach YOUR measure of success and conquer life. Once you truly come to understand the message and connection between love and individuality, you will understand the importance of living a transcendent life in a state of grace for yourself and others.

Throughout this book you may come across repeated messages; healthy repetition is a tool you should have in your toolkit and keep on your tool belt. That is because you need to hear them, understand their importance, and convince yourself to first change your mind and then your mind-set. In turn, your cornermen will help you prepare for, step into, dance in, conquer, and survive the ring of life. Know that you are not alone in feeling pressure that you don't belong, that you're not measuring up, missing the mark, or that you are falling off life's course; you're just going through the mining process. Let me ask you . . . Ever wonder what is the measure and whom you're measuring up to? What mark are you missing, and who set it? What is the course, and why must you be on it? That line of questioning is your witness. You know in your spirit that your measure, your mark, and your course are uniquely yours. You know in your soul that you are a diamond in the rough waiting to be uncovered. You may be covered by dirt and hidden for now, but your time is coming. Diamonds are formed by pressure. Tune into your channel, think divergently, connect the dots, and manage your reality. Once you have been discovered, pressured, polished, and the true you made to shine through divergent thinking, your possibilities will be endless. It's your time to emerge. Seek and you will find your path. Get busy conquering life and shine unapologetically. As friend and fellow author Kristy Morrison would say, *Make Life Happen*! Chart your course and define YOUR path! Love the Skin YOU'RE in!

Chapter 1

THE DIVERGENT SOUL: GOING AGAINST THE GRAIN

"The very nature of People is something to be overcome."

—Steve Jobs

Dear Society,

Have no fear. Difference is here! Difference is our core strength and the superpower that dwells within us. Difference is nothing to fear. Welcome it. Value it. Celebrate it. Difference is truly the spice of life that walks among us!

The morning started off cool and brisk with a gorgeous sunrise over the Potomac. As I peered out the train window on my way into work, I remember contemplating my life journey with a smile on my face, appreciating every experience that had brought me to that moment. I exited the Metro in military tight formation with the rest of the crowd and made my way in to work. I walked the long halls to my office in my power red suit feeling particularly well that day, until I encountered a male colleague. Instead of, "Good morning, Virginia. You look particularly happy today," I was greeted with a surprised look, followed by a once-over and "Red suit . . . huh? Bold choice." My initial thought, "Thanks! Go bold or go home." If I had not personally witnessed his body language, heard his tone of voice, and seen his facial expression, I might have taken the greeting as a compliment. However, it was clear to me that the red color of my suit triggered a conditioned response about its appropriateness in the workplace. His training and cultural conditioning delivered a negative association to his mind upon seeing me, which could not be reconciled with anything other than alarm bells because it was different and out of the norm for a woman in the workplace. You see, red is often associated with rage, anger, danger, power, boldness, romance, and all things scarlet. But red is also the color for joy, courage, energy, strength, vigor, willpower, determination, action, vibrancy, passion, radiance, love, and leadership. Why did my choice that day cause a hiccup in his? Perception. His singularity in thinking could not see past his conditioned mind.

There is a concept in Chinese philosophy known as *yin yang*. It describes how seeming opposites, or contrary forces, in the universe are interconnected, complementary, and interdependent, working hand in hand to produce favorable energy rather than oppose each other. While they are individual parts, they are one and give rise to each other as they interrelate with one another as a dynamic system of assembled parts. Simply put, one force is favorable, or differently referred to as masculine, while the other is negative, or differently referred to as feminine. Neither is preferred nor is better than the other, and both are highly desirable factors when they exist in perfect harmony. This construct of equality between negative and positive factors is of course contradictory to most existing fundamentals where one or the other is forever sought in its absolute form. However, the yin and yang concept advocates the necessity of having both factors present for the ideal. Physical manifestations of this can be found throughout the sciences, philosophy, and other aspects of life. We see this duality and very concept in tangible examples as day and night, fire and water, shadows and light. For subscribers to the philosophy, everything has yin and yang aspects, even social models of responsibility. So, why is it that when it comes to established archetypes, finding harmony in duality (yin yang, or "normal" and different) is a foreign concept (pun intended)? Somehow this ancient principle has been challenged to make itself readily available or stretched to social concepts and ways of being. The usual norm when faced with dualities in society creates conflict that yields a lack of equilibrium. Fear is paired with paralysis, restricting the flow of favorable energy and thus causing unfavorable reactions.

Looking at this concept of opposites attract, let's consider it in terms of grammatical construction. We call it a lack of reconciliation when two forms of negation (the same) occur in the same sentence: a double negative, leaving us with an unfavorable reaction. To leave it as such or to support the incorrect construction is unacceptable, and the student making the mistake would receive correction. For the sentence to be a sentence (society), it must be constructed of interrelated, interacting, and complementary parts, or opposites (individuals). So, why do we overwhelmingly change the precept and accept it when applied to social ideals? Society tends to see a norm and something different as the double negative offsetting harmony and intensifying the negation with manufactured perceptions of irreconcilable differences. The coexistence of dualities is seemingly insurmountable. Why? Because individuality (difference) is not valued within the collective. In the conditioned mind, value lies in fear, and fear will keep you from discovering your true likes and dislikes.

Every society is built upon a foundation that establishes norms and expectations of behavior through social conventions and constructs. These social norms identify accepted rules and roles of conduct—how to react and not react, what's appropriate and inappropriate—for given social situations and gender. They have even gone so far as to adopt conventions like protocol and etiquette guides to further establish written rules, procedures, methods, values, and belief systems for conduct. These constructs usually carry the majority, all-or-nothing view and have found their way into societal settings as well as affinity groups and cultural communities. Why is such importance placed upon norms? They are a way of establishing a controlled identity, a way of being, a sense of belonging, comfort, and expectation. Just as governing tools, social conventions are organizational tools utilized to maintain societal order, hierarchy, privilege, and boundaries. Archetypes were developed to support this conditioning, and we are taught these behaviors from birth. Fear of missing the proverbial mark guides our effort to measure up. Social conditioning plants the desire to look, act, think, and be like everyone else—to conform to the norm as if a mindless drone. Outside of a military environment or a life and death situation, though, it can provide a false sense of security and belonging, lulling participants to sleep and leaving them defenseless against the swings of life. Take, for instance, the seemingly harmless gender role life-cycle models for men and women:

> *A male is expected* to exhibit athletic prowess from an early age; play with cars, video games, and sports figures; be physically fit, handy, strong, tough, and fearless; go to college and be the best; graduate and be the best in their chosen field; find a wife; procreate; climb the "corporate" ladder to the American dream; make a lot of money; provide for and protect his family; and win at everything.

A female is expected to be delicate, docile, and dainty; play with dolls, pom-poms, kitchen sets, and to dress up; study and master homemaking; be smart but not too smart; go to college and find a husband; get married, have children and take care of the home; and if she has a job, it should not be too demanding; she should ignore her capabilities, sacrifice her dreams, and be content with her "station" in life.

If this cycle is your choice, then it is your choice, but make sure it is YOUR choice. If it is not your choice, defy categorization! In an interview with Kristy Morrison, author of *Make Life Happen*, she cautions against following the norm or the status quo:

It is definitely an area that creates a lot of pain for people. They don't understand why they're not as happy as other people they see around. They're not connecting with their inner self. They're not realizing and following that path or journey that's going to guide [them]. Everyone has a purpose and everyone has a journey. It's just that if you are following a system or a guideline that someone told you to do, you're never going to be authentic and find yourself because you're just too busy listening and following someone else's journey.

Social expectations have largely paralyzed us into single ways of thinking and conditioned our minds toward prohibitive gender patterns, when we should see and recognize each other for who we are. There is nothing to fear by doing so. That strong, chiseled man may want to be a nurse, gymnast, or cheerleader and not an athlete or firefighter but still chooses a "manly" role. The gorgeous, vivacious woman chooses to be single, professional, artistic, educated, cultured, strong, fun and the boss instead of a homemaker. In the former scenario, he loses himself and his identity. In the latter, she conquers life but faces consequences for her divergence from model expectations.

Gender roles, class, race, religion, and other identifiers are culturally ingrained and program people's thinking and behavior. Not only are they fundamental constructs of society but they are also tools that allow for the creation of categories and classification. Institutional reinforcement and practices in the workplace, at home, and in social settings perpetually reinforce them. The challenge to you as a member of society becomes not to allow others to project their biases onto you. It is difficult. Objectivity goes against our nature, as we are inherently biased to our experiences and associations. Our minds consciously and unconsciously form biases. Anyone or anything outside that experience would be challenged to convince you otherwise.

What all of this comes down to is the innate conflict between society and individuality and its source question: how does an individual thrive and find success in a collective society? Let's look at this type of thinking using a monologue delivered by the character Jeanine in the screenplay *The Divergent Series: Insurgent,* in which the writers brilliantly depict this conflict between society's conditioned thinkers and divergent thinkers:

> Now, two hundred years later, we are all of us living proof that peace is indeed attainable. The reason for this is of course our faction system: Erudite, Dauntless, Amity, Candor, Abnegation. In dividing people, according to personality and aptitude, we've created a society in which each faction plays a critical role in maintaining the social order. But this harmony we've achieved is now under attack from a small but extremely dangerous group of individuals. We call them "Divergents." They are in essence the worst of what humanity used to be: rebellious, defiant and uncontrollable . . . These divergents despise our system because they're incapable of conforming to it.

While this is a fictional work, the correlation to real struggles of humanity is uncanny. Apart from gender, race, and ethnicity, personality traits and aptitude are often utilized to identify and segregate; however, these things alone do not a society make. So why is it even a consideration or why is there a need to bring these things into conformity according to categories? Viewing the whole in parts that prevent the intersection of those parts negates the whole. It's not a matter of bringing peace or togetherness, nor even of facilitating effectiveness or efficiencies in living or governing. Case in point: the turbulent times we find ourselves in today. Taking such a position is about power, about setting and maintaining a status quo. It is about asserting one's will over another's, ironically due to subconscious fears of inadequacy, justification, self-preservation and/or self-hate; all are born from weakness and not from a position of strength. In our example, Jeanine's argument is built on fallacious reasoning and gives no contemplation of root causes, only scapegoats in the relentless quest for control over the many. When such a suppressive stance is taken, you not only deny your own individuality but also that of others. You are choosing oppression over free will.

This type of assembly-line thinking ignores individuality in the creating of society and inherently breeds conflict. According to Kristy Morrison, "Those under this mindset tend to ignore the signs and decide to be happy with what they have, even when life is challenging them trying to guide them to happiness in their individual purpose." Meanwhile, on the other end of the spectrum, such a paradigm that is rigid in its application and thinking is a double-edge sword pitting member of society against each other in a power struggle or in the justification for existence. In the not-so-far-fetched-from-reality fictional trilogy *The Divergent Series*, based on Veronica Roth's written novels, we witness the turmoil caused by well-intentioned "socially conscious" motives in which people of like aptitude, character, and values are separated into factions to ensure peace and heal humanity. Individuality is completely ignored and discouraged, leading to feelings of suppression, oppression, disenfranchisement, lack, and self-hate on the part of group members within the same society. Meanwhile, divergent souls like Roth's main character, Beatris Pryor, try to hide their differences to fit in and feel safe, which creates inner conflict for them. Beatris eventually follows the pull of her nature down its path and connects the dots to her purpose, while simultaneously learning to love herself and conquer life. Don't miss the metaphor for the action. The underlying message is about life. When social constructs manufacture reality and do not fit, civic responsibility lends itself to two choices—fight or flight. You can throw the fight, flee, and lose your identity, or step into the ring and fight to survive and conquer. Imagine how different the world would be if such divergents as Jesus, Harriet Tubman, Abraham Lincoln, Amelia Earhart, Martin Luther King Jr., the Tuskegee Airmen, Nelson Mandela, Elizabeth Cady Stanton, Robert F. Kennedy, Barbara Jordan, Mahatma Gandhi, Severo Ochoa, Bill Gates and so many others had not lived and walked in their space. They did not flee their purpose. The lives of these divergent souls teach us invaluable lessons in freedom, authenticity, and the greatness in being who you were meant to be for the shared purpose of humanity. The path will always have a price, but if you move in the spirit of humanity, the societal byproduct has potential of historical proportions and reward for the greater good.

Open your mind to reality, and you open your mind to possibility. It is illogical to expect all human beings to be the same or to subscribe to the same life formulas; nevertheless, most do, buying into accepted societal notions without question and following prescribed patterns. What if we changed the narrative by starting with a look at our inner self and questioning our fears? What if we all took an inventory of ourselves and honestly asked the question "Am I a part of the solution or the problem?" It is not too late to revisit the sins of the fathers and correct them; however, atoning is a choice. What if we could find the yin and yang in ourselves and others, the differences yet commonalities, and accept them? We would be able to tap into the vital energy and focus needed for healing communities. In Chinese medicine, the healers or sages focus mainly on getting back the right balance of the factors in any given scenario, identifying which force is dominating and in fact causing the imbalance to occur in the first place. The end goal is to regain the fundamental principal balance of factors in conflict, while identifying a suitable style of treatment. What if that style of treatment were learning and practicing an adaptation of the six main principles in the yin yang relationship in society and organizing structures? What if . . .

. . . *we accepted everything has its comparative opposite or other and practiced tolerance?* No one thing is complete without another. The seed of its opposite is a part of its existence.

. . . *we all understood that we were interdependent?* One cannot exist without the other.

. . . *we understood that our different parts give us greater strength and dimension?* Difference completes the circle of the whole and proliferates capability.

. . . *we were all our brothers' and sisters' keepers and selflessly supported each other?* Humanity continuously changes, and when we fail at managing our reality, we negatively affect each other. Too much negativity eventually consumes and weakens the whole.

. . . *we became love and an extension of others?* Transforming ourselves to see the other side of the coin through the eyes of others provides perspective, understanding, and sociocultural exchange.

. . . *we saw ourselves in each other?* The fear of seeing ourselves in another is to learn that we were wrong. There are always traces of one in the other.

Fanciful, perhaps . . . but something to contemplate and aspire to. The point is that rarely is difference encouraged, and it is too easily relegated to a back burner. What is the root cause? Conditioned thinking that wants you to only see life a certain way. That is why a woman wearing a red suit in the workplace offends; why a child is bullied because of their intelligence; why an interracial couple strikes a nerve; why lives are extinguished for religious beliefs; why an African American as president is intolerable; or why the mere thought of a female running things is unthinkable. It's all conditioned choice. But, if conditioned, is it really choice? Time for a pulse check . . . are you in control of your thinking or is someone else?

The time is always right to do what is right. Going against the grain may initially feel like an unpopular path but divergent souls live there, so get comfortable. Separate who you are from who does or doesn't like you. You look different, you walk differently, you talk differently, you express yourself differently. There is nothing "wrong" with you. You just hear your own music and march to a different beat; you have a divergent soul. Rejoin society. Reprogram your mind and learn to view social norms as guidelines, instead of as expectations. You are not in competition with anyone but yourself. Then, and only then, will you be able to find YOUR path to conquering life on your own terms. Do not move through life unhappy, feeling judged, trying to reach standards set by others. View success as individual and qualitative in nature, not through the lens of quantifiable measures. What is success for one person is not success for another. Trying to fit into uncomfortable shoes will always cause discomfort and pain. You simply need a comfortable pair of shoes and permission to be who you were born to be in this boxing ring called Life. Just like diamonds, we are formed by pressure—pressure that we are not measuring up, that we are missing the mark, that we are falling off life's course, or that we must conform. Take heart. You are capable and ready to shine. The road less traveled can be a lonely path until it's not. It's your choice. You can choose to settle for merely adequate, or you can choose who you were born to be and achieve excellence. Choosing mediocrity to dull your capabilities or hiding your difference so as not to offend, in order to appear normal, is not an option, and those who love you should not let you do that. Why be a copy, when you were born to be an original? Love the skin YOU'RE in!

Chapter 2

TRAIN UP A CHILD: THE CREATIVE PROCESS

"Let's raise children who won't have to recover from their childhood."

—Pam Leo

Dear Society,

Train your child to be who they are, not what you want them to be. We all have a purpose. It's on us to find it.

How we view the world is influenced by how we come into and exist in it. We are born, live, and die, with most people never really living, much less finding and walking in their purpose. The cares of life are easily distracting and lead us from our path, intentionally or unintentionally. Those cares start with our caregivers and their conditioning. While it is true that the combination of predisposition and parental upbringing are the two greatest shapers of a child's future, genetic excuses only go so far. That child will eventually become an adult and must account for his/her own actions. Nurture will be a determinant.

Nature and nurture are always in play with living beings. One, the other, or both are at the heart of every concern, every decision to have and raise a child. Making that choice is a tremendous responsibility and one of humanity's greatest fears. If parents are motivated too far one way or another (e.g., too strict, too lenient), a child can be ruined for life or much of it. Some do not take the responsibility seriously enough, others as if the child is an iteration of their own life, while others try to control every aspect of the child's life as if a possession. None of these scenarios meet the necessary requirements for setting the foundational principles paramount for conquering life. The truth is first-time parents have no clue how to be parents and rely on input from their parents, social circles, research, and observation. The problem here is that your parents and friends were first-time parents and are conditioned based on their experience; they will advise you according to that. You also bring your own biases based on what you liked and did not like from your childhood. Second- and third-time parents set their standard of measure by the first or the second child and try to correct perceived missteps, instead of understanding and meeting that child's individual needs. Children are not clones and raising them should not take a manufacturing approach.

The difficulty here is trying something different, as opposed to how you've been brought up. Subconsciously, it calls into question your upbringing and conditioning, which can be a difficult pill to swallow and hard thing to admit, so it is rejected. Moving outside your comfort zone when you are already uncomfortable is like skydiving. It's a fear most people will never overcome because it is not viewed as a necessity. On the contrary, it is more than necessary to raise children who will have no need to recover from childhood experiences. It requires a summoning of strength to do what you've never done before—to move outside of your comfort circles and conditioning to ensure you and your child are exposed to the diversity in life. You will have opposition, proverbial naysayers, and persecutors, but you will also find enlightened, like minds and support. The only things you will lose are redundant cycles, negative energy, biases, and dead weight with so much more to gain. If you train up a child in the way they should go, that child will not depart from that path. They may go off-script in their creative discovery of life (and that's okay), but they will eventually return to foundational principles, think for themselves, and stand for others. If you don't train that child, and instead allow others to do so, that child will break your heart.

So where do you begin? Foundational constructs like familial order exist for a reason, but not for a reason that smothers or stunts growth. Life is discovery and should be viewed as a creative process. As in the case of a child coloring outside the lines of a design that is given to them, the creative process must come from somewhere and not necessarily be void of structure. However, structure should not exist for structure's sake. Whether it comes from something that exists or is in the mind's eye, it has a source. Why is it that we never seek to understand that source? The question is never asked of the child who colored outside the lines, why they did so. Conditioned responses have taught us to assume that the child lacks the ability or a skill set. Basically, Jack or Jill is not measuring up to the status quo. Allow them to test their budding gifts through exploration, self-discovery, cross-cultural experiences, and exercises of both left and right brain characteristics. Such exposure can combat identity crisis, uncertainty, and fear of oneself and others. Worrying about a child being like everyone else will cause them to be like everyone else and not be themselves. The methods by which we measure and condition children ignores the essence of individuality and abandons the creative process of life. Well intentioned as we may be, there is tremendous difficulty in avoiding the tendency to live through our children, instead of raising them and teaching them how to be individuals. Your hopes and dreams for your child's life may not be their hopes and dreams. Children were not meant to be clones or tributes paying homage to their parents. Every person born to this earth has a purpose. It's on each of us to walk our path and find it. Listen to and support your child. In addition to structure, teach them identity and confidence through exploration, discovery, and engagement. Children may be born with identity, but they are unconscious of it until it is cultivated. For those charged with the temporary care of children outside of parental care (e.g., daycare, school, camp), the responsibility is just as important; children not only come from you but through you. Some people are purposed to help nurture, raise, and train them. I call these individuals "the village." No matter how they come into your life, they are precious gifts ripe for unconditional love. Give it to them, place them on a right path, and watch them soar. Place them on their path and allow them to spread their wings through exploring boundaries that are part of a flexible structure. Whether in familial, educational, or peer relationships, it is extremely important to counter this flexibility with an understanding of discipline, roles, rules, and why they exist.

To be clear, I do not advocate children run households. They are children, and stages of growth clearly reveal a lack of knowledge and experience to execute that duty. Furthermore, they do not have the capacity to raise themselves; that is the job of caregivers. In addition to biological parents, parental figures can provide security for exploration and growth while offsetting potential damage. The village surrounded me, lifted me, supported me with time and love, and picked me up while I was learning to fly. The village brought diverse perspectives and experiences to my table, as well as provided guidance and a safe space to train and hone my childhood whims and passions. My village helped to instill discipline, morals, values, faith, responsibility, motivation, determination, work ethic, and strength in character and purpose. The village exponentially improved my chance to conquer life.

Children respond to and mimic what they see. How an authority figure meets life and responds to challenges or crisis is how a child will learn to respond to it. If a parent overreacts in tone and body language to a child bumping their head on a table, the child will cry, ingrain that response, and associate every similar experience to it with the same reaction. If the parent chooses not to respond in an overly emotional way and reassures the child they are ok, the child's response will be less emotional and will be short lived. Teaching children what it looks like and means to overcome and how to endure, two main prerequisites for conquering life, can only benefit them. The psychological growth that occurs in the preteen and adolescent years is critical to equipping or handicapping young people. Attitudes and actions will imprint and determine their altitude. The village experience sets the tone. Be mindful of what you imprint and allow others to imprint.

Many of us are products of divorce and carry that brokenness throughout life. Divorce is not a reflection upon you, so reject a spirit of brokenness. If you've never been told, it's not your fault. Choose empowerment instead of defeat. You may have issues. Acknowledge them, work on them, and then work them out. You can still be more than a conqueror and teach your child how to be one too. Use your experiences as lessons learned for motivation and impetus to change. Raising a child is not meant as a way for adults to figure out what happened in their life or to work it out through the child, which usually results in a lack of parenting and a dysfunctional friendship. Be concerned with providing good parenting, and the friendship with your child will inherently come with a greater reward for both of you. A friend cannot be a parent, but a parent

CAN become a friend. You may not realize your child is internalizing all of this, but they are—to their detriment. Do them a huge favor and don't transfer your hang-ups to them. Messed-up parents can seriously mess up kids. As the saying goes, hurt people hurt people. Consider just some of the ills of our society—selfishness, hate, intolerance, bigotry, racism, sexism, prejudice, and cronyism. All of these are taught and learned behaviors, derivatives of hurt people, their insecurities, and narrowly lived lives. Too much exposure to any one thing or to any one way of thinking can have damaging consequences. The excuse, or the false reassurance, that "they will eventually grow out of it," or "they are just going through a phase," or "they are just fine. I was exactly like that" may or may not be true and are unhealthy and potentially loaded stances to take. They also suggest denial and detachment. Be conscious of and remain plugged into your child's feelings, friends, and involvements without hovering. Insight into your child's well-being can prevent detrimental scarring that can hinder their personal and professional lives as an adult.

When health and well-being are discussed with regard to a child, it is usually in reference to the physical body; however, mental and emotional health are just as important if not more. If children are going to grow into healthy, functional adults, it's important to take a proactive approach and be mindful of their holistic growth and well-being. There are many ways to address concerns, whether by traditional, holistic, or recreational practices. The important thing is to address them. There is absolutely nothing wrong with going outside the family to do so. Find the most suitable option for the circumstance. Don't leave children to fend for themselves. A negative emotional state of mind can directly affect all levels of the physical state of the body. It's the basic idea of yin and yang and the principals of harmony and balance. These concepts should be of concern even in childhood so that they will not be a struggle in adulthood. Lifestyle practices that we normally reserve for adults are just as important for children. Lay the groundwork, but don't go crazy (remember, all things in moderation). To ensure optimal growth and development, health and wellness must be in alignment. When an imbalance occurs in an element, it becomes the weak link and the point where unraveling can occur in the otherwise complete cycle.

The easiest place to start for growing children is the physical. Physical exercise and extracurricular activity are vital, as well as nutrition and sleep, for heart health and mental and emotional wellness. While you might not want your child to miss out on the fun of unhealthy "kid" eating, think about incorporating that euphoria as a treat or reward incentive and make sure they have a healthy diet. Contrary to popular belief, that does not have to equate to expensive if you get creative and resourceful. It does take effort, and your child is worth it. Involving them in individual team and team sports will keep up their appetite and help successfully maintain metabolism while teaching them team building and transferable life skills in several areas, including coping with competition, disappointment, loss, and sportsmanship. The point of extracurricular involvement should not be whether you have a prodigy on your hands. If you do, great; talent will manifest itself immediately or soon thereafter. The point is a healthy, well-adjusted, coordinated, fearless child ready to step into the ring of life and take on the world as an adult.

To prepare children for the world, mental health and strength must be a focus. If their mental state is not intact, it precludes all else. Let's first clarify the difference between mental health and mental illness so that you will know how to proceed in concerns of wellness. Mental health refers to overall emotional well-being, and mental illness to specific disorders or problems. If you are dealing with mental illness, your creative process will look different but it will still be creative. The variance will be greater considerations and possible limitations in how you proceed.

Nevertheless, even little ones deal with stress, and stress can take you out of the ring early. Regular physical activity will help reduce those stress levels. According to Carl Brown, licensed massage therapist, wellness coach, and father, "It's important to realize that children internalize more than we do and carry most of it in their minds. Adults tend to have more options for outlet. Unlike children we also have experience on our side (if that's saying much). They have not been exposed to situations or have the same frame of reference." Fear, abandonment, rejection, and the like are all stress and anxiety triggers that can send them into their own tailspin. Whether the sign is visible or invisible, you will be able to tell if something is affecting them. Watch their behavior patterns. Do your best to keep negative energy away to avoid imbalances. Using methods such as yin and yang color therapy can help bring about mental healing, with certain colors invoking certain emotions to usher in different mental states (colors have their own energy levels). Also monitor their attitudes and mind-set. Help them keep their feelings in check through productive ways that favor mental health and stability. Some experts recommend practicing techniques such as meditation and hypnosis with children, and you definitely want a professional involved if you consider this route. The goal of all of this is an awakening of the brain to learn to send messages to the body to calm itself (captain and crew, which you will read about in chapter 4). The brain has the necessary positive energy thoughts to remove all negative thoughts and replace them with relaxed energies. The conscious simply needs to connect with the subconscious.

Mind-set and emotions must be kept balanced. Children may heal faster than adults physically but their mental healing can be precarious. In an interview with attorney Cris S. Houston, she shares how she has been able to remain confident and resilient throughout her life despite her challenging upbringing:

One of the reasons that I remain strong and resilient is that I believe in seeing a therapist when I am going through life. Several of my psychologists have asked me, "Have you always been the strong and resilient person that you are now?" The people, the women, who raised me really built my self-esteem. They validated my strength and my self-assurance and my confidence. And they gave me permission to be strong and to have higher self-esteem and to believe in myself. I needed it because I grew up in an abusive household. My father was verbally, physically, and emotionally abusive. I now know as an adult it was because of mental illness. I had daddy issues, my parents divorced, and my mom moved to another state and she wasn't around. But even so, there were others who built up my strength . . .

Emotional well-being is tied directly to a person's mental state and can be affected by many things, from family dynamics to schoolyard bullies to self-inflicted anxieties. Ms. Houston went on to provide a further perspective on bullies, "Growing up I learned that people have to find a 'flaw' to make themselves feel good, particularly when you're athletically inclined, academically inclined, attractive, charismatic, or any other different thing they are not and have to question. They are transferring and projecting their feelings of inadequacy or failure onto you." Taking this a step farther, we can say that children channel their parents and their behaviors. Educate your child about these things and teach them how to counter factors that cause stress and anxiety with basic techniques as deep breathing to relax tense muscles and create a more stable emotional state. Also, watch for emotional eating. This could start an unhealthy trend. You cannot protect them from everything in life, but you can prepare them. Stress, a byproduct of emotional issues, is scientifically described as electronic pulses (energy) that connect to the brain. The chemical changes produced by negative emotions produce negative destructive energy, such as anger, frustration, overexcitement, self-pity, grief, and fear. Emotional wellness is nothing to play with and you should involve a professional when you see trouble escalating. Children need to be taught healthy ways to express emotion. Examples to the contrary confuse them, so take care with what they see and hear in their environments. Teach them to talk it out by talking it out with them. Don't allow them to find their solution by locking themselves away in their room, burying their heads in video games, or going on hunger strikes or self-assigned diets. They are children. While you want to give them a voice, theirs is a voice without experience. Find opportunities to let them practice decision-making on their own and how to manage that emotional equation, but provide some oversight; know when times are appropriate and when they are not. The skill of successfully working out their emotional choices as well as paying attention to physical health and spiritual development will ensure their emotional stress levels remain at a healthy point.

Raising children is a creative process; don't pigeonhole them. It often takes a village to raise them and that's more than okay. Give them exposure to different environments. We are not born with self-esteem, and the familiarity of exposure will help that deficiency. However, we are born with an inherent concept of love, an open heart, and open mind. Without nurture, the right encouragement, and experiences in life, that can change and not for the better. Counter life antagonists by promoting the most powerful of all emotions—love. Live family values of respect, honesty, patience, acceptance, integrity, accommodation, forgiveness, and wellness. Children must see this and other positive, healthy demonstrations of love, self-worth, interactions, and teamwork. Exposure to these things will engrain into their subconscious and teach them to love and respect, not fear, their individuality or that of others. Socialization and acculturation should start at home but does not stop there. Teach them not only how to maintain individuality but also how to interact with and go in and out of different situations and cultural experiences. In today's society, this is no longer an option. Understanding how to do so and being comfortable in doing this is not selling out one culture for another, as some with limited minds may think. It is, rather, accepting your place in the world and buying into an investment with humanity. Life does not merely exist for your sake in your home, community, racial category, or socioeconomic bracket. How uninteresting and what a waste that would be. Educate your child and expose them to living. While education may not be the solution to everything in life, it is an important microcosm of life that not only provides a foundation and opportunity for exploration but also opens doors, hearts, and minds.

Not everyone will grab opportunities that come to them, but that's not the point. The point is to give your child an opportunity and a fighting chance in life. From there, it is their choice, so let them have it. While you can still influence them in the critical years, listen deeper than the surface to what they are trying to communicate to you. Sometimes parents tend to jump onto the next thing without giving enough time, energy, and focus to what has been said or already started. So be patient with your child's development and pay attention. If you have raised them with surrounding values such as scholarship, service, and diversity, trust and allow the creative process to take shape. When you train your child to be who they are and not what you want them to be, that child will respect you even more for it. Give them guidance and let them go. No matter the pitfalls, trials, or tribulations they encounter, they will have the tools necessary to become more than a conqueror in life. They will love the skin they're in!

Chapter 3

ANYTHING BUT NORMAL: SURVIVING AND THRIVING

"If you are always trying to be normal, you will never know how amazing you can be."

—Maya Angelou

Dear Society,

    Who defines normal and why do we buy into it? Living is anything but normal. The world shuns divergence from the normal, but I encourage you to embrace it. Normalcy precludes individuality. What if we all met life with courage and vigor to be who we are and accepted each other for it. What if we all got busy being anything but normal? Then we would all be living and not merely existing.

While we may have had a routine as a child, life was anything but normal. Make believe and ascribing different personas was the place we lived. "Normal," as pertaining to personality or a way of being, was not a consideration. But as we travel through life some of us start to feel different, not quite comfortable in our own skin, like we don't belong, or even like outsiders trying to fit in. I recall feeling trapped or suffocated by social norms and expectations, when my spirit knew those norms and expectations were not meant for me. That was because I was different. You are different and were meant to be so. We are outside of the norm. The cookie-cutter approach has never worked for us, and our very essence yearns to release its individuality. This was a constant pull at me and, honestly, an unsettling realization to me, particularly with those around me putting on their best cookie-cutter imitation and the white noise of social expectations surrounding me.

We start training for life at a young age, whether we consciously realize it or not. The challenges I faced, caused me to grow up faster than usual. As an only child, my faith and scriptural mantras were respites in difficult times. Extracurricular activities provided welcomed distractions, while the words of poets like Robert Frost, Ralph Waldo Emmerson, Langston Hughes, and Maya Angelou were a refuge. When I could not make sense of my world, their words did. The ultimate form of healing was a combination of them all and my life companion—music and the gift of singing. Plato could not have been more accurate when he said, "Music is a moral law. It gives soul to the universe, wings to the mind, flight to the imagination, and charm and gaiety to life and to everything." These words were light to my soul and gospel. Through them I desired to be their prophet. It was this early exposure to music and the performing arts that provided the ultimate willing suspension of disbelief that strengthened and helped carry me to and through each challenge. Come with me on my journey. Let's start from the beginning . . .

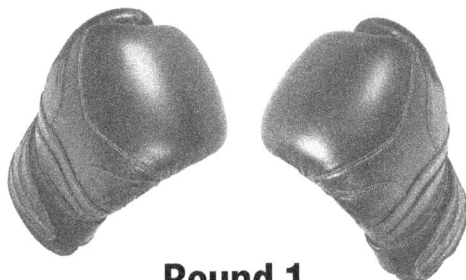

Round 1

Early Childhood Discoveries

On a November evening at the Youngblood homestead in the little historic town of Goliad, Texas, my mother woke up with labor pains. My father was quickly summoned from his favorite old juke joint called Bland's. He, my grandfather, and great-grandmother rushed my mother thirty-some-odd miles to Victoria, Texas, where she would give birth not long after to a spritely and chunky baby girl—me. Little did we know what life had in store or my true purpose.

Our home base was the countryside of Goliad, population fewer than 2,000. I was raised by my mother and extended family, while my father was literally off to the races: Daddy was a jockey. Mom and I traveled with him until I was about two years old and the rat incident occurred. Dad was riding for the J. B. Ferguson ranch in Mackay, Texas, where our family stayed in a big red barn inclusive of a kitchen and bedroom. One day, a rat the size of a baby kitten wandered too close to me and sized me up for the mother lode of meals. Thank goodness, Mom was alert and on top of the situation, or I might have been rat food and you would not be reading this book! All of you who are mothers can imagine her reaction—that was the end of us living on the Ferguson ranch and traveling with Daddy.

My early years were mostly happy and carefree like those of most kids raised in the country and too young to realize their family struggles. Both Mom and Dad worked full-time. My great-grandmother and great-aunts mostly saw to my upbringing during the day, until I was about age four and we made the big move to the "city"—Victoria—where life and its lessons introduced themselves. By age five, I had already learned lessons in the importance of faith, the value of life, the fear of absence, and both the loss of material things and innocence.

I felt a call to baptism as a three-year-old and was baptized by the late Reverend J. S. Smith at St. Peter's Baptist Church. As I started down the aisle, my mother moved to intercept me, thinking what led me was a childish whim. My great-grandmother stopped her, advising her to let me be and reassuring her that I knew what I was doing. What I was not consciously aware of at the time was my immediate need for a hedge of protection around and over me. This walk of faith is my most vivid childhood memory, where I remember moving in purpose. I answered every question asked by the pastor clearly and precisely, declaring my love for the Lord and desire to be baptized. Lessons in the value of life came not long after.

One sunny afternoon, I sat on the concrete steps of our country trailer house enjoying Spring. Then, suddenly, my German shepherd and best friend appeared leering, salivating, and snarling at me on the roof of our car, just feet away. I still do not recall how I escaped his bound my way in apparent madness, but I did, and my father had to put him down. That was my first loss. Shortly after the biggest scare of my mother's life occurred. I was playing in my room on the far end of the house, jumping up and down on my bed as if on a trampoline. My closet doors were open and from inside I heard a rattling noise. My curiosity, of course, was piqued, so I jumped down to inspect. As I reached for the rattle on the upper end of the "coiled rope," something stopped me and caused me to go ask my parents if I could play with my new rattle toy. They immediately knew what the rattle was, and my mother kept me from returning to my room, while my dad grabbed a shovel from outside and chopped off the head of the rattlesnake. I had never asked to play with a toy before and had no need to ask. What made me ask that day? Because of the response of my parents, I did not experience fear, but in the transference of spirit came to understand my value to them. To this day, my mother recalls that incident with chills and thanksgiving for God's hedge of protection around me.

Dad was gone a lot. I remember waking up groggy and wandering through the house to locate my parents, like children do, only to find an empty house. Fear struck me for the first time and, in this case, introduced itself as foe. Panicked and feeling absence, I ran to a neighbor's home for refuge. When my mother returned minutes later from quickly driving my father to work, she panicked and set out to look for me. Our reunion was full of tears and joy, and is likely the reason she keeps such a close eye on me to this day, even across thousands of miles. The absence I felt in the pit of my little stomach was real, and I never wanted to feel that again. Unfortunately, I would later experience a comparable feeling to absence—loss.

Not long after, I endured two traumatic losses. 1) My favorite baby doll and new best friend went missing at a laundromat after we drove off and forgot her, and 2) Our family was locked out of our home and lost everything—one minor looking back, but nonetheless a traumatic event, and the other quite traumatic. Regarding the latter case, I will never forget the disbelief, pain, sadness, fear, and strategy (all at the same time) on my mother's face and in her voice, nor the sight of her trying to find a way in, crawling through a window to salvage necessities and a few toys while reassuring me everything was okay. Everything was not okay. Life was seriously screwed up and trying to break her and take me out of the fight. I was emotionally on the ropes and needed a break.

After losing the trailer, we moved to temporary housing. My father retired the first time from riding and returned home to work in the oil field, while mom drove forty-plus miles or so to teach. During the day, I stayed with a sitter who had a son in his twenties. I was four years old. My mother came to pick me up one day and noticed blood on my panties. When she asked me what had happened, I did not answer. I do not believe I knew how to answer. It was not a matter of feigning ignorance but of my mind protecting me. I do not believe I ever returned to that sitter. Years later when she brought it up again, my only recollections were an uncomfortable feeling, a man approaching me, confusion, pressure, then nothing.

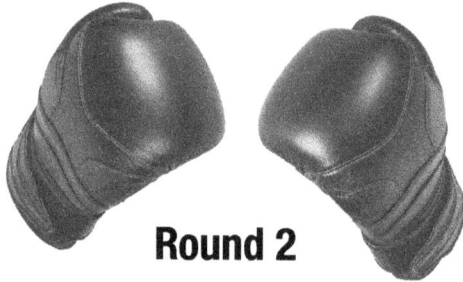

Round 2
Grade School Promise

Now a retired educator of forty-three years, my mother sacrificed a great deal to give me a solid developmental start in education, socialization, and acculturation into society. It was clear, early in my childhood, that I was anything but normal. I just didn't know what that meant, and it didn't feel like anything I wanted to be. Like any child, I was conditioned by parental teachings, beliefs, and habits; however, I was always connected to my individuality but chose to hide it most of my life. The funny part about hiding difference is that you really cannot hide it, particularly from those closest to you. Even though they may not call you on it, in their spirit they know, because spirit recognizes spirit. My capacities not only in academic achievement but also everyday living and processing were heightened— emotionally, physiologically, and spiritually. I was creative, athletic, and artistic, and I had an unconditional love for people. I was a little girl who loved life, classical music, musical instruments, fishing, crabbing, swimming, and sports of all kinds. I excelled at everything. I was inquisitive, I processed information quickly, and I was always eager to meet any challenge and succeed. It was not about the people around me or about a need to prove anything to anyone, but rather a conquering spirit that burned bright early. My mother realized it and did everything she could to cultivate it.

I grew up under the watchful eyes and discipline of the nuns and teachers at Nazareth Academy (affectionately N. A.) for my formative years. They were the extension of my village, for which I am eternally grateful. At Nazareth, I experienced an extension of the discipline taught at home, in addition to discovering and developing my talents, aptitude, and growing in faith. We did a full day of reading, writing and arithmetic as well as studies in the arts, sciences, and extracurricular activities. It was at N. A. that I had my first crush, flourished, excelled at band and sports, and learned to accept people for who they were—all God's children. It was a utopia, until it wasn't.

Even during these years, my mind had the uncanny ability to sort and reconcile conflict in a way I could not understand at the time. Sucker punches caught me unaware and taught me the unexpected lessons of difference, manipulation, politics, choice, and to expect the unexpected. My paradise was shattered when my athletic prowess was discovered and certain parents preferred my skills be used on the basketball court and not as head cheerleader. My parents and I were reassured something would be worked out. However, deals were struck and my course changed. These backroom dealings did not sit well with me, so much so that I begged my mother to leave the Academy. I transferred to Patti Welder Intermediate for seventh and eighth grades.

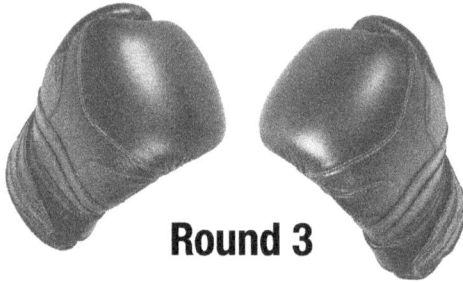

Round 3

Preadolescence Blues

I shone to an even greater degree in academics, sports, and choir at PW, though I learned some of my toughest lessons, involving bullying, discrimination/racism, competition, and cliques. Perhaps the most hurtful was my introduction to racism in my first romantic relationship, when my boyfriend suddenly stopped communicating with no explanation to me. I later discovered that his parents were fine with us being friends but not fine with us dating because of our racial difference. Never mind my talent, personality, aptitude, or potential. Social norms, even in the 1980s, frowned upon interracial relationships. This devastating experience crudely opened my eyes to this societal sickness as well as prepared me for other racial-profiling incidents I would be subjected to that year. Admittedly, this round was a rude awakening and had me on the ropes a bit, but I kept my wits about me and kept my feet moving in the right direction, barring bitterness from my heart. It was difficult to do. The lesson in difference followed me from N. A. to Patti Welder and created yet another situation in which I was on the receiving end of discrimination and bullying.

I was different and I knew it. From my intellect and aptitude to my speech, carriage, and reaction to certain situations, I was different, especially to others who looked like me. My peers would purposely look for things to try and present me in a bad light. For instance, I acquired the nickname "Light-Bright" because of the shiny illumination off my forehead from oily skin. Cliques would start rumors, pick arguments, and threaten fights. Competition was no longer confined to the court or track but quite literally experienced in every facet of my life outside of sporting arenas with boys and girls alike.

Transferring to public from private school expanded my world and taught me an invaluable lesson of divergence. People fear what is different and what makes them question themselves. My thinking, behavior, intrinsic motivation, and life exposures were different from the norm and became a threat. In response to what I discovered, I tried to dial myself back to fit in at school and only allowed myself to exhale in the privacy of my bedroom. High school introduced a new degree of loss, grief, and trauma, leading me to spend the latter half of my adolescent years playing chameleon while being angry at the world and acting out.

I am not sharing all of this for pity or in competition for a "who had it worse" dialogue. Stepping out of denial to acknowledge bad and traumatic life experiences is the first step to healing and being able to overcome. I had great times running dirt races and tasting victory; taking victory laps with my dad on horses after winning races; making mud pies; frying an egg on the concrete steps of our trailer; flying kites; picking wild blackberries with my mother; and growing a watermelon patch under our porch stairs by spitting out seeds into the fertile soil. I experienced a host of joyful childhood experiences, but the challenges and lessons learned from surviving and thriving were integral building blocks for who I would become. The mere fact that I survived childhood without irreparable damage and with exposure to the good, the bad, and the ugly began to build my strength and inform my ability of how to overcome. No matter how hard parents try, they cannot protect their children from life without keeping them from living. Joy and sorrow are never far apart. We must learn how to interact with them. Looking back over my life and seasons of change, I have come to realize that life has no coincidences. Everything happens for a reason. Once you get out of your own way and find your way to this perspective, you will have your "Ah-ha" moment. The pieces of the puzzle will start to fit, followed by acceptance of your journey and forgiveness for yourself and others. Forgiveness is a gift, not a chore. Acceptance is a powerful thing. For those who find it, enlightenment is life transforming, and its gifts are liberation and empowerment. The journey may be a scary thing and call your world into question; however, the destination is a beautiful place to arrive at and much more rewarding than trying to fit in. I cannot think of a more fitting summation than that of the character Edith Prior in *The Divergent Series* for a wake-up call to respect and accept individuality:

> Hello. I come from outside the wall, where we have all but destroyed each other. We designed your city as an experiment. We believe it is the only way to recover the humanity we have lost. And we created factions to ensure peace. But we believe there will be those among you who will transcend these factions. These will be the Divergent. They are the true purpose of this experiment, they are vital to humanity's survival. If you're watching this now, then at least one of you is proof that our experiment has succeeded. The time has come for you to emerge from your isolation and rejoin us. We've allowed you to believe that you're the last of us. But you're not. Mankind waits for you with hope beyond the wall.

Normalcy is overrated and is stress living. It impedes individuality. Then why try so hard to be/feel normal? The world may shun divergence, but I encourage it. Your normal should be based on no one else but you. Life is not merely a show but the ultimate prizefight. It's the epic battle that brings everything except mercy; winner takes all. Unleash the fighter in you. The ring of life can be brutal and debilitating, with body- and head shots from every direction at a rapid pace. Stay off the ropes and out of the corner; fight your way out, if necessary. Channel your fear into strength. Learn to step away from the right jab and counter with a left hook; keep your feet under you and dancing. If you get knocked out, get up before the final count. Take a knee, if you must, then stand up and shake it off; you're okay. Keep your gloves up and step to it. Draw on your spiritual strength for supernatural stamina and ability. You can take and absorb the punishment. Tie up when you need to but don't back off; keep the pressure on. You cannot conquer life by playing small or by taking a normal approach.

To conquer will require combination skills—patterns of hooks, punches, jabs, and crosses. Fire the jab, stick and move. Circle from around the jab to the left because life knows your strength is in your right hand. Counter with a left hook and work the cut. To find YOUR eye of the tiger, you must be anything but normal; it is your strength. Your opponent will know what is inside of you by the face you wear. Keep that challenger in front of you in perspective and remember your training as you face life. Embrace who you are and the potential within. Life will require you to be "more than" to conquer it. Accept and love the skin YOU'RE in!

Chapter 4

PREPARING FOR THE RING: TUNE INTO YOUR CHANNEL

"It is not the mountain we conquer, but ourselves."

—Sir Edmund Hillary

Dear Society,

Be convinced in your heart and mind that good things are set aside to make way for great things to arrive in your life. You can't do that from the couch. You must train to build stamina, endurance, and strength of mind. You're never going to become who you were meant to be until you prepare. Your answers lie in the ring. Remodel your mind-set and face life head-on. Be you and no one else!

The world is a much more complicated place than most people are comfortable believing it is. We fight to stand; we fight to develop; we fight to be who we are; we even fight to simply exist. These are all bouts of life, so recognize them as that and start preparing for the ring by tuning into your channel and being brilliant at it. Challenges will come and are supposed to come to mold, shape, and guide us to our path. The problem arises when we are unprepared to meet life. We easily succumb to the chains of its mental training as a means of survival. With clouded minds closed to other possibilities, we learn to love our safe and familiar chains—an irrational state made rational. They are a known quantity, and a jailed mind will accept anything, including subjugation and lack. Freedom, for some, will be a difficult process, but nothing worthwhile ever comes easily. The only way out is through. Reprogramming your thinking will transform and change your way of being. Reena Dayal, author of *The Brilliance Quotient*, would encourage us to listen to what we are drawn to instinctively in tuning into our own channel. In her *Love the Skin YOU'RE In* interview, she emphasized, "When you want something, if you are clear about thinking what you want, then chances are that you will get it because your mind will make decisions that will lead you toward it. It might not happen the way you want it to but it does." She admits being challenged to love the skin she's in for most of her life, particularly from a very literal sense. She had to challenge her own limiting beliefs and assumptions:

> I grew up with a thing about me not being beautiful because I grew up in a culture whereby dark skin was looked down upon. As a child, these things impact big time. Sometimes we look for beauty and we look for things to make us happy outside us. It's time we look inward and see how beautiful we are. When you become consciously aware through conscious discipline of who you are, not just me waking up one day and saying this is who am ... but through challenging beliefs, challenging assumptions, listening to your inner voice, fine tuning intuition ... when you do all of these things and realize who you are as a person, one is super powerful

and truly much more wiser and greater. Sometimes, we have to dig beneath all of these layers we have grown up with through life, through what society has told us, what other people have told us, what life experiences have told us to get down to who we are. Knowing who you are as a person, and that is *The Brilliance Quotient*. You are then your own benchmark . . . and you do not have to rate yourself against anybody else.

To be the fighter you need to be to withstand social pressures, reclaim your individuality, and conquer life, you must first conquer your mind. Change it and your mind-set, and you will be able to tune into YOUR own channel and block out the white noise of life around you. First, get to know and draw upon your natural strengths and master them in this endeavor; play to your strengths. They will guide your path and take you to where you need to be. In *The Brilliance Quotient*, Reena discusses the importance of nurturing your intuition. She asserts that while some may be naturally gifted in this ability, and can weed out the plethora of noise that is typically in our minds serving as a distraction, others can develop mastery. "When you nurture your intuition, you start connecting the dots to various things and circumstances in your life. We draw things to our life; there is no such thing as coincidence" (Dayal). Until you reprogram and train your thinking, you will never rise above your lowest level of belief; what you believe is what you will achieve. Boxers are expert at this. The fear of not conquering the ring is the strength they draw upon. If they lose a bout, they come back stronger, quicker, and wiser for it. In addition to physical training, they also train their minds to not fear their own greatness and to meet their full potential. They face every challenger with courage and channel their fears. Mohammad Ali was perhaps the greatest at doing this because of his holistic approach to training and discipline involving the mind, body, and soul. At the heart of Ali's personal success in and out of the ring was his mastery of the inextricable connection between the conscious and the subconscious mind—the singular duality of the human brain with two distinct minds.

Perhaps one of the best analogies for understanding the singular-duality function is the captain and crew example. Every ship has one captain. Your conscious mind is that captain. Your conscious decisions determine where the ship goes. Every ship also has a crew of hundreds to thousands. Your subconscious is the crew. That crew, so long as it is properly trained, follows orders and carries out the will of the captain. The crew does whatever the captain says. The captain does not pilot the ship. The crew does. It is the crew's job to maintain the ship and keep it on course. The captain provides the orders. However, a conundrum presents itself with the proverbial chicken-or-egg question: Who is in control? The captain or crew? We are completely subject to our subconscious because it carries out what the conscious mind says, hears, or thinks. The subconscious mind never sleeps, and it constantly reinforces whatever words or deeds you repeat the most. The crew will always say "yes." If the conscious mind is undisciplined, the subconscious mind will be even more so. Any effort by the captain to regain control will be a struggle or be futile. In the article "The Subconscious Secret," by Scott Sulak, author of *Get Your Ship Together*, he explains, "If the captain wants the ship to go a different direction but fails to properly communicate that information to the crew then the ship will be headed in a different direction than the captain wants and he becomes captive by his or her crew."

More often than not, this is our circumstance, particularly in the teenage years. Bringing the mind and emotions under control is more than a notion and is truly an undertaking; however, only once we come through those circumstances can we truly begin to understand and embrace the prophetic words from Invictus, "I am the Master of my Fate, I am the Captain of my Soul" (William Ernest Henley).

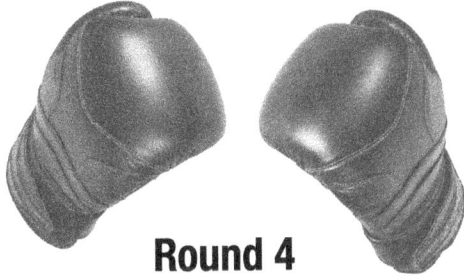

Round 4

Senior High Shade

My parents divorced at the end of my freshman year, sending me down a potentially destructive path of juvenile behavior of partying, drinking, doing disappearing acts, and engaging in associated behaviors. To deal with my anger, I began to conform to social norms and expectations. To fill the void of my father, I started looking for love in all the wrong places, save perhaps one. In addition to setting myself up for life's blows through bad, emotionally driven choices, I had gotten good at wearing masks. I am quite sure that I am responsible for my mother's beautiful early gray hair. Balancing my mind and emotions wasn't even on my radar. The fighter in me was on the mat for the count and the captain was on her way to abandoning ship with the crew on a crash course. However, by the grace and mercy of God and the training instilled in me, I managed to maintain a facade of control, in true chameleon fashion. I channeled my energy into "old faithfuls"—education, choir, sports, and other extracurricular activities—to keep my mind quiet and focused.

Without reprieve life challenges kept coming for me. I bore the death of six friends between my junior and senior years, including my best friend and boyfriend, as well as the loss of others close to me. My world was almost unrecognizable by graduation. To say that I was ready to leave Victoria for a fresh start was an understatement. Life had me on the mat, almost out for the count, and gasping for air. But it was the "light" inside me that burned brighter, lifted me up, and helped me see the way forward. With my eyes almost swollen shut, I was bloody but unbowed. Regaining my willpower and finding my strength to stand, I realized at graduation that the masks I had been wearing were suffocating, and that the forays into social circles were attempts at trying on the lives of others to avoid my own. It was now time to live my own life. I made it through high school, managed to maintain my academic performance, and graduated at the top of my class in a virtual four-way tie for valedictorian. I may have been bruised and battered but I survived, was stronger for it, and determined to thrive. That round taught me that life is messy, that love hurts, that choices have consequences, and that loss is permanent. More importantly, it reinforced who I was and Whose I was. Crossing that graduation stage, I was more than ready and eager to move on to the next phase of my journey. I was ready to tune into my own channel. I understood the power of difference. My mind was changed, and I was ready to change my mind-set.

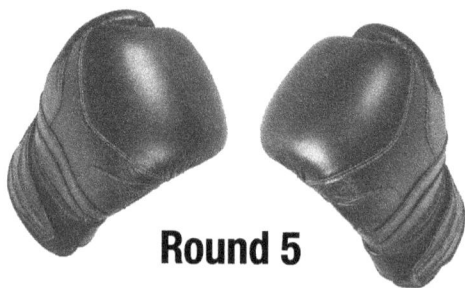

Round 5
College Dreams

I left Victoria with a puff of smoke behind me, not necessarily because I was running from anything but instead because I was running toward something—a rematch with life. My mother and stepfather loaded me up in Uncle Finlay's truck and my car and took me to Baylor University in Waco, Texas. Baylor started off "all that and a bag of chips," as we used to say to express our excitement and pleasure with something. I met my best friend and ride or die for life there in the first semester of my freshman year, as well as fell head over heels at first sight (but it was complicated). Baggage I thought I'd left behind relocated with me. Apparently, I was still looking for love in all the wrong places and found it. However, there was something different—my mind-set. This time I was more prepared for the ring. I felt the freedom to pick and choose my bouts; nothing was going to be hoisted on me unless I chose it. Unfortunately, I neglected to inform my subconscious about the gaping voids of love and acceptance in my life that it was still trying to fill from my parents' divorce. It might have helped if I had been consciously aware. The great news was that some healing had taken place. So, this relationship was not the center of my world.

I embraced my newfound independence and involved myself in everything I could. Sophomore year, I was the juggling queen pledging Delta Sigma Theta Sorority, Inc. and Mu Phi Epsilon Fraternity simultaneously. Sleep and I were strangers. I was in a zone. Grades remained on point, and everything was clicking. It was the beginning of me discovering and being me. I had been in search for that freedom and acceptance for some time. Delta and Mu Phi were the doors of opportunity to find my channel. In Delta, I was drawn to the strong, polished, diverse, visionary, trail-blazing and divergent-thinking women among her ranks as well as her history of service and of leading change. Mu Phi drew me into a higher musical calling and understanding of the performing arts in my life. The two together were transformational and transcendent for my life and have played integral roles in the path that I have walked and connected dots. However, prior to that I had become disillusioned with the university and escalating racial tensions on campus. Simultaneously, I was seeking funding opportunities to continue at Baylor, but the administration was uninterested in retaining a 4.0 student among their ranks who contributed positively to the campus. On my confiding in one of my former choir directors, she recommended me for an audition with the choral director at Southwest Texas State University (now Texas State University–San Marcos). I stopped there on the way home that Christmas for an audition and left with my education paid for and a new alma mater. While I had every intention of graduating as a Baylor Bear when I left home, life had other plans for me and I unknowingly began to follow them.

SWT was like magic. Whatever I put my hands to turned to gold. My sorority sisters and music fraternity family adopted me with open arms and without questions. It was at Southwest that I began to clearly recognize and embrace certain abilities, aptitudes, and leadership competence. My time there allowed me to tune into my channel and lay foundations for the next phase of my academic, personal, and professional development. See, what most people rarely process or miss about their college years is that it's about more than academic performance. Yes, I really said that. Academics, of course, is the priority; however, your college years are the first opportunity you truly have to discover who you are, what you're about, identify clues toward your purpose, and break socialized chains through your studies and interactions with a diverse population that is also moving forward in this exploration. It is the first time in your life that you can choose for yourself and begin to define your path in life.

With that freedom, you must determine your risk tolerance. My father was a jockey, and his risk tolerance extremely high. My mother an educator, and her risk tolerance was extremely low. Unsurprisingly, I fall in the middle on the high side. Whatever your level of risk tolerance, it can serve you well or badly by empowering or paralyzing you in reaching your full potential in life. At the time, I was not thinking about all of this. I was too busy striving for perfection (something none of us will ever achieve) and subconsciously trying to prove something to everyone. I had tied my worth and identity to my performance. The captain was sending detrimental orders to the crew. Those daddy issues persisted and were clinging to me tough. Nevertheless, SWT was an environment where I could and did thrive. I had mastered the uncanny ability to press forward and bury my troubles. I am not sure the latter was healthy, but it was a means to an end that I would later face and overcome. I recall thinking, as I neared and, later, after my graduation, as I completed my last recital, received the Outstanding Senior Award, and prepared to be both commencement speaker and soloist, "What's next?" I was so busy creating the dots that I had no clue where to place them and how they connected to create my way forward. The dialogue running through my head was, "How can I, Virginia LeBlanc, not have a clue?!" Well, of course, it was a blow to the ego but a healthy, eye-opening one. While I began to feel the pressure of not having a plan or knowing what was next, it made me susceptible and open to destiny. I'd gotten so caught up in the white noise of social norms, constructs, and expectations that I was unprepared for what would happen next. This was my first conscious encounter with my divergent soul and opportunity to exercise my divergent spirit. Nature and nurture now intersected.

Rounds 4 and 5 taught me to be open to a new course and not fear life's challenges, but instead to expect them. They are necessities. You must be open to change. That's how we grow. You must go through something to learn how to overcome something. You must go through something to find and tune into your respective channel.

To tune into your channel requires a decisive attitude to guide and direct your path but also to let go and trust. Did I mention that life is ironic? Take for example the captain of a ship who gives the orders but, at the same time, must let go and trust the crew to carry out the orders to fulfill the mission with or without his physical presence. How do you get there? Self-awareness, acknowledgement, and examination, as well as an understanding and acceptance of reality and the world around you are just some of the ways. Glen Gibbs, author of *Remodel Your Mind-set*, reminds us that there are only a finite number of ways to interact with others and the world around us. We interact based on the five traditionally recognized methods of perception, or senses: sight, sound, smell, touch, and taste. In an interview conversation with Gibbs, he shared, "If we understand the source of how different information affects you, you can understand how to redirect your presets in your mind-set." Understanding that your emotions are tied to certain senses that trigger memories and bypass your conscious mind, empowers you. The senses trigger automatic responses. You must learn how to counter these by finding those things that reinforce positivity into your life. One of my go-to redirectors is music. Sounds can trigger memories and take you to a good space, forcibly realigning your mood and emotional thinking to a rational and unaffected place of forward-moving options. From Gibbs' perspective, in other words, the goal is "to help you remove the mystery around" tuning into your channel, so that you may work on mastering it. Once you remove the mystery and become self-aware, you will be amazed at what you can conquer. You can conquer life itself!

Peers, authority figures, and even loved ones can deposit information like a virus. If you are caught unprepared, your system will be altered or infected and destroyed beyond repair. Learn to think for yourself and tune out the white noise of other channels, unless it is good programming for you. If you do not do so, you risk thwarting or prolonging your journey. Constantly check and address your mind-set. Mind-set affects performance. The best news? You can always do something about it. Change it. Don't be afraid of change in career or personal development. New beginnings give us a clean slate and new opportunities. Set and manage your own culture, and learn how to operate in it while existing within the norm. Want to give yourself the best advantages in life? Learn what people value and appreciate. Study and learn people—how they think, what they think, and why they think it. Apply and practice this. You will be amazed at the results! This skill set will be invaluable to you and to your success as you move through life.

You are what you think. Program it or be programmed; get rid of old programming. Failure to do so is not an option if you want to conquer life. Listen to what you say to yourself. Your words are ingrained into your subconscious, which is even more powerful than a computer. Your subconscious will self-fulfill the prophecy of the words you speak and think before you realize it. If you say you are a failure, you will be a failure. If you say you will never be happy, you will never be happy. If you say you are petty, you will be petty. The mind is powerful, so stop feeding it junk and don't allow others to feed it junk. Turn your words positive and they will become your way of being—positive. Mind-set is a powerful yet vulnerable thing. The subconscious mind is a goal-striving mechanism. Filter in, filter out. Rid yourself of limiting thoughts. What you say and hear is programmed into your subconscious. The only way to reprogram it is through spaced repetition. Tell yourself, "I am beautiful. I am great. I can do all things ..." Remain clear that this is not an exercise in flattery but in reprogramming your thinking and tuning into your channel. Just because something is handed down, doesn't mean you have to take it or continue hurtful traditions. You don't have to accept lack, defeat, struggle, abuse, addictions, depression, and other generational hand-me-downs.

Visualize and see your way through breaking the mental chains of society—biases, prejudice, privilege, naysayers, bullies, and misguidance from the well-intentioned. It all holds you back. Let go of the cares. Learn to forgive yourself and others for imperfections and conditioning. This is a priority and a must. Too often people carry hurts, hang-ups, and bad habits into adulthood. Parents do the best they know how, but they are human and sometimes impart unhealthy and destructive messages to their children. This reality holds for a time, but at some point, particularly as adults, we must put away the things of our childhood and take responsibility for ourselves. An unfortunate number of people allow things that have been done to them to stunt their growth and potential in exchange for nursing harmful ways and perspectives. Don't be one of them. They may dwell in anger or denial, but you don't have to. Both will blind and destroy you. Face and deal with your issues, make your amends if possible, and get on with living. Figure out who you are without that dead weight. Learn and accept the truth about yourself, then put that newfound knowledge and way of being into practice.

As Rodolfo Menjivar conveys in *Life Balance*, "We are doing the best we can in the moment with what we know." If you hate something, change it. Don't dwell on it. Move to action! Your heart health and sanity depend on it. Find shelter and rest in your Higher Power, and, in turn, that power will give you peace and strength. Don't let dysfunction limit you and your potential. If you do not put a stop to it, it will most certainly stop you. Stop looking at the outside and instead look inside. It's the inside that cripples you. Break the negative cycle and spirits holding you back. Be a chain breaker and a difference maker! When you really get tired of being sick and tired of losing to life, you will move to action. We know a tree by the fruit it bears. A tree either springs forth with life and growth or it withers and dies, due to the seeds planted, the root system, or environmental conditions. It is either the victor and a fruit source in the chain of life, or it is a victim. Choose your surroundings wisely, plant the right type of seeds, and root yourself deep. Put yourself in the best conditions to bear healthy, life-giving fruit. It all starts with the mind. Don't feed insecurities. Once you learn to respect and love the skin you're in, insecurities will fade and conquering life will become a natural fit. Tune into your channel and not the white noise of social expectations. Love the skin YOU'RE in!

Chapter 5

DIVERGENT THINKING: THINKING WITHOUT A BOX

" . . . Two roads diverged in a wood, and I—
I took the one less traveled by,
And that has made all the difference."

—Robert Frost

Dear Society,

Life is jazz—a living, breathing, constantly changing tune. The important thing is to not get caught up in the plan. The plan might cause you to miss your solo. To successfully play the tune requires an open mind, vision, spatial awareness, instincts, grounding, flexibility, and improvisation. It requires divergent thinking. Live the jazz life and live life without a box!

W e often get discouraged and do not see how the dots are connected, due to social constructs and the white noise of expectations around us. Life experiences, how we think, and the paths we choose play important roles in our journey, discovery, and outcome. What is seemingly not connected in your mind is, but without discovery of the other part, the big picture will not come to pass until the right time. You simply need the keys to open endless possibilities to your world. Muhammad Ali once said, "The man who has no imagination, has no wings." If you want to change the trajectory of your life, you must think differently from the norm. You must free your thinking. Until you learn to access this superpower, you will never be able to overcome social conditioning so that you may define your own path. As we get older, our thoughts about what is possible become more and more limited. Tuning into your channel, reprogramming your mind, and learning to control and redirect your thoughts are necessary steps to help you tune out the noise of society and connect the dots to achieve your purpose.

Children innately explore and exercise this gift. Remember the child who colors outside the lines? She is already exercising her superpower. Her little mind has not been exposed to the systematic conditioning involved in traditional educational models. Her imagination leads the way in her world, and it is one without limits or restrictions to a dominant hemisphere of the brain—right or left. Her mind is free and clear of impossibilities and will continue to be so until it is guided toward one or the other. At some point, she must choose . . . or must she? Perhaps she is the next Picasso, Christa McAuliffe, or Major General Marcelite J. Harris, and she sees something that we cannot, because it is not our time to see it. Coloring outside the lines with a different spatial awareness is a part of her journey and her way of connecting the dots subconsciously and finding her purpose. Outside forces that interfere with that process just because she is "supposed" to be coloring inside the lines, interfere with the creative process and her discovery of who she is and what she is capable of. What is the fear here?

That she won't be like everyone else? That is a gift, not a burden. While some might reach for explanations of teaching order and discipline or other sociopsychology reasons for enforcing adherence to lines, structure, and the like, we miss a key opportunity to ask the child "why" they are coloring outside the lines. We more readily instruct them to return to the lines and chalk it up to justification that they have no artistic talent, didn't understand the exercise, or that they are simply being rebellious. It was always difficult for me to color inside the lines of what most people who look at a coloring book drawing would consider the central focus. Even as a child, try as I would, my mind would always go to the big picture and work inward. By doing so, I had more options in approach, color palette and combinations, creativity, and the ability to change my mind before arriving at a central focus of the picture as I saw it. If something was missing, I would add it. My divergent little mind was already at work, marching to the beat of my creative little soul. But as I moved further into the educational process, I had to color inside the lines to get the grade and be promoted as "normal" for that grade-level competency.

As adults, we spend time setting our mind right and conquering the fear of life and potential outcomes. The risk tolerance for most people is extremely low and the fear extremely high. Therefore, our need to control the situation is off the charts. As children, we have no concern about the world. It is all about individuality and exploration. There is no need to set our mind right or to conquer fears. We are fearless, until we are taught to think inside the box and learn fearful behaviors. Our personalities and aptitude then become shaped and determined by that box. Before the child realizes—and often that does not happen at all—their life is made so much more difficult out of fear and our own personal restrictive training. There is no fault here, just incorrect thinking. Childhood is the perfect opportunity to foster divergent thinking in problem-solving and discovery. In the ring of life, that is what we do. Learning to think and view life and your circumstances apart from the norm is an asset. It allows you to be aware of what's inside and outside of the box, but gives you the choice to not choose either in your decision-making process. It enables you to have the ability to walk your own path and choose the road less traveled, which will make all the difference. You become the "influencer" and not the "influencee." Your decisions become your own, with the consequences resting on you and you alone, but it's okay because you understand that life is a living, breathing, constantly changing tune. Like a jazz number, you cannot get caught up in the plan. The safety and social conditioning of the plan can cause you to miss your solo and most certainly limit the brilliance of it. If you're going to be the original you, you must get comfortable living the jazz life. Like boxing, the beauty of jazz is the organic experience—the ebb, the flow, and the skills required. Both call for a fusion of the sciences; the performing arts; the physical, mental, and spiritual on full display, with training in discipline, judgment, deduction, accuracy, agility, creativity, recovery, and understanding of the opponent (another boxer, your own mind, or a musical key). This is divergent thinking—the means of possessing presence of mind while having absolute, undiminished recall and control at your disposal for conscious and subconscious creative and analytical solutions that determine and guide your decision-making process. Operating with this ability is invaluable. Plans will falter, but when you set up your plan like a jazz chart, you have room for improvisation. The outline is there, giving you some structure, but so is the opportunity for something more—divergence.

If the line of the plan gets away from you, divergence will allow you to riff until you find your way back, one note, one dot at a time. Divergent thinking facilitates a 360° view of life—what is before you, what is behind you, and what exists on the same plane as you. It involves strategy, intellect, and forethought. It is your other cornerman next to perspective. Some people may try to relegate divergent thinking to a growth mind-set, but it is not. However, the growth concept can be a catalyst in its development and application. Divergent thinking is dynamic and ever changing. It reveals more than one way to think about, overcome, and conquer an obstacle or challenge. It is the single most powerful concept, strategy, and tool for conquering life.

Some people are natural divergent thinkers, hardwired from birth (nature), while others must learn through experience and conscious effort to program the crew (nurture). For learners, the usual routine is the familiar, which is the enemy of divergence. Experience has taught you to make guarded choices in how and when to view and do things, from finding a seat in a room to choosing the best time of day to drive to avoid the most traffic. You will choose the same seat and the same time, every time, without a thought to other possibilities. To tap into the greatest power of divergent thinking, it is necessary for there to be exposure to and development of different activities, practices, and processes that train both hemispheres of the brain. Strive to develop in different directions:

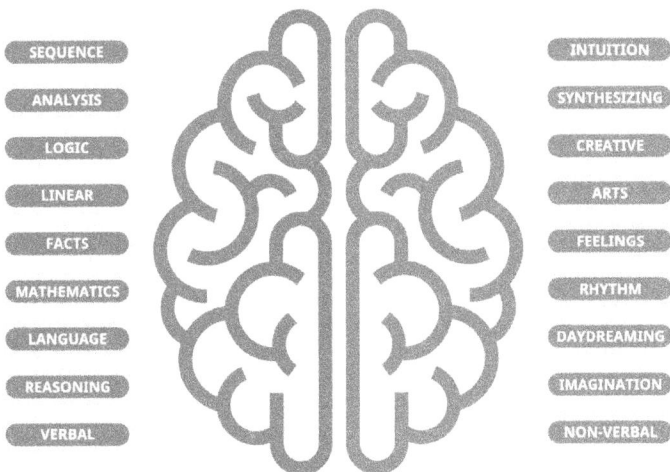

L E F T BRAIN RIGHT

LEFT	RIGHT
SEQUENCE	INTUITION
ANALYSIS	SYNTHESIZING
LOGIC	CREATIVE
LINEAR	ARTS
FACTS	FEELINGS
MATHEMATICS	RHYTHM
LANGUAGE	DAYDREAMING
REASONING	IMAGINATION
VERBAL	NON-VERBAL

As children, we are already tuned into our channel and readily available to access both right and left brain thinking. We do not think in halves, nor strengths and weaknesses. As adults, this is more challenging but not impossible. One must identify the holes and seek to fill them through experience. Most holes will be in the right brain (an argument for the importance of the arts in education). To realize the full potential of divergent thinking, you must identify with, marry, and constantly employ both halves of the brain. Be open to not only creative, diverse, emotional experiences but also academic, logical, and analytical experiences to put the pieces together and connect the dots on your life path.

ANALYTICAL vs. creative

While advocates of risk aversion encourage staying inside the box (left or right), and others encourage thinking outside the box (still right or left but outside), I say think without a box. Blow up the whole paradigm! Yes, this may be a scary concept at first. Society has conditioned us to think inside the box, and education teaches us to think outside the box, but life will teach you to think without a box. The box exists to keep you in or to keep you out. Often, you cannot even see the box, and then the paralyzing question becomes, "What box?" In divergent thinking, mind-set is more important than the how and the skill of thinking. The subconscious mind is a billion times more powerful than a computer. It is observant and analytical. It notices and processes the body language of those you encounter. It takes in knowledge but doesn't allow it to influence the objective unless told to. If you are unable to shift your mind-set, your vision will become clouded, your perception off, and fear about your course or the outcome will set in. Your state of mind (conscious, the captain) and mind-set (subconscious, the crew) control your outcome. Without your emotions under control, skill is useless. Your strategy when facing Goliath, in whatever form or fashion, will be triggered by a fight-or-flight response. It is common for most people to flee and shrink under the towering shadow. However, when the choice is to flee out of fear, divergent thinkers become Goliath. Divergent thinking will allow you to channel your fear into strength, and the thought "I don't have problems, just challenges" will be your war cry and first nature.

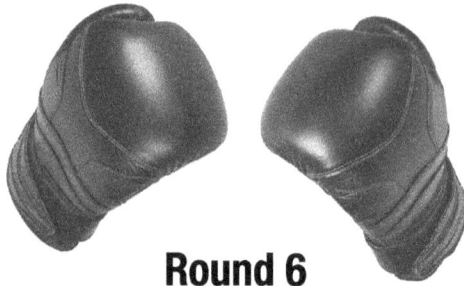

Round 6

Postgraduate Quandary

I was a graduate! But not knowing what was next or having something locked down was a jolt to my system and sent me into "fight" mode. With my back against the wall, I went to the big picture and worked my way toward the inside. I decided to start a graduate program in music, with studies in higher education administration. Why this route? At the time, I had not connected the dots but knew I had a passion in one and interest in the other. I also had to figure out how to pay the rent, and there just happened to be an opportunity in Greek Life. I began to move into action and favor moved with me. I was named to an assistantship with Greek Life and began to apply the knowledge I had gained over the years in an effort to resuscitate and reorganize the local council. I also decided to apply to the music programs at Rice University and Northwestern University and was accepted to both. However, financial packages and constraints seemed to be closing those doors to me. Meanwhile, a window opened for my forward course to Indiana University.

One day I called on business to the national headquarters of the National Pan-Hellenic Council. I left a message and received a return call from the executive director, Dr. Michael V. W. Gordon, at Indiana University Bloomington. Not only was Michael the executive director of NPHC but he was also a professor of music education at the Indiana University School of Music. We discussed business having to do with the NPHC at SWT, and then the conversation drifted to our common musical backgrounds and my potential future at IUB School of Music. Floored, I graciously accepted Michael's offer to connect me with individuals of influence there at the school. What Michael did not know, and the irony of it all, was that I had just discarded an application to the School of Music. True to his word as always, he connected me right away with such individuals as Dr. James Mumford, who became my mentor, surrogate father, and champion, as well as the incomparable Martina Arroyo, my sponsor and first voice teacher at IU. I immediately acted on the referrals but was disappointed to learn that the last audition for the coming academic year had already taken place. However, the voice chair at the time offered me an audition opportunity, should I be able to make it to the faculty meeting the following week. The following week?! It was already Wednesday, and I had to prepare and be there by Wednesday of the following week, not to mention I didn't have a flight!

I walked with my voice teacher and pianist, sharing all that had happened and my interest in auditioning. As I did so, I felt my excitement waning at the realization that I had no means of getting there, until my pianist came to the rescue, offering to transfer her frequent-flyer miles for a small price. In less than two weeks, my life and trajectory changed, simply because I chose to fight instead of flee and followed my diverging path to the next dot instead of the safe and comfortable action of remaining at Southwest. I made my arrangements, prepared my mind and mind-set, and stepped into the ring. The ring was not without challengers, but I found my way through each one. It was clear that Bloomington was the next dot on my path. Making the decision to remain at Southwest not only allowed me to be present for the right time but also enabled me to gain the experience and transferable skills I needed to walk through the open door. That following Fall, I was a master's student at Indiana University School of Music, starting the next and most transformative phase of my life.

I discovered that sometimes it is necessary to be removed from everything we know and love so that we may be molded and shaped according to our purpose. The next three years did just that. They were about making new connections, finding myself, persevering, and learning to let go. This time, while there was a fear of the unknown, it was a different type of fear, moving in strength and with resolve. Being alone in Indiana was a mental and spiritual awakening for me. It was the rebirth of my divergent soul and where I discovered the true me—strong, intelligent, diverse, adaptable, wise, and tried by fire. I knew I was meant to do and be more. I knew that I was different and that Bloomington, Indiana was my launch pad for discovery.

When you channel your fears, and move forward in strength, your senses will heighten and you will be able to see your way over, under, around, or through the wall, whether you have an ideal view or not. The point is, you can see to find your way. It's a matter of programming a healthy mind to understand that you simply do not have problems, only challenges. You will overcome those challenges one way or another as you employ divergent thinking practices. You simply must find your willpower to find your strength. Perspective IS everything. What you think is what you will believe. You are only as capable and strong as your belief. If there are confines in your thinking, your belief will be weak. Life is unpredictable, so prepare yourself and develop your toolkit of divergent capabilities. Holistically cultivating both hemispheres of the brain toward instinctual responses for problem-solving and discovery will make you uncompromisingly ready to face life, suppress your fear, and anticipate potential threats in walking along your path. Break the chains that bind your thinking and put yourself in the driver's seat. Watch the change in how you think about what to do and how you respond to situations, even those seemingly outside of your control. You will no longer react based on emotion but out of necessity.

Dr. Yolanda Holmes, of Washington DC Dermatology, is a consummate example. Sharing a bit of her divergent story with me, she revealed that she had always been interested in medicine but didn't discover her love for dermatology until she was exposed to the field through a series of appointments with a dermatologist in her last few years in high school. She had difficulty applying to medical school due to a lack of exposure to preparatory needs and deficiencies in knowledge required for successful admission. She did not get in at first, so she decided to take an alternate path, the post-bac route, which prepared and qualified her for medical school. Dr. Holmes says about her decision, "I was excited to take an alternate path. It helped identify deficiencies and strengthen them. I thought, 'This is an opportunity for me to improve myself, to do better, and to find a way, even though I was told no, to find an alternate way to be accepted and go to medical school.'" She went on, "Dermatology is very competitive. I did things which made me more attractive, even though I didn't have the best grades. I was a research fellow, which helped me get into the program, among other things." Dr. Holmes realized, as I have come to realize, that "no" is a "not right now" when you know you are tracking your purpose. So, keep after yours. She used what resources, knowledge, and experience she had to scale the wall through divergent thinking and continues to utilize the strategy in her thriving practice.

Divergent thinking will not only teach you how to face and resolve difficulties but it will also allow you to see a greater number of options from varying angles as well as learn how to accomplish foreign tasks through inference. It enables you to move away from convention, like teaching yourself code and how to build different kinds of websites based on inference. When the two halves of the brain are working harmoniously in know-how, whatever the situation, plans of action and execution may come together in a way that may even surprise you. You may become supremely conscious and aware of yourself. You may notice an increase in recognition, response time, and resourcefulness, allowing you to know what you know and know what you don't know more quickly. Someone may tell you what they want you to think, but you will be able to immediately see for yourself the holes in their argument. If you're out surfing rough waters after a storm, you are able to do so not just because of skill but also because you have the ability to make quick assessments and divergent decisions as to what's going on all around you and decide whether or not to catch the first wave or the second. Your scientific analysis and understanding of the laws of gravity tell you that if you get caught in a rip current, you should go with the current instead of fighting it. Simultaneously, your right brain will tell you to look for a floating object until you can recover or be rescued. Divergent thinking is like having the best of two worlds, which you can turn on or off, pick and choose. You can choose to bat left or you can choose to bat right.

Like a sailor, you can spot and chart course with your left brain, then flip back to your right to successfully navigate the waters of life. We are the only species on this earth that can evaluate and determine what we can do and what the outcome will be. We ARE different and were meant to be so. Animals use their brain for survival within their environment. However, the difference between a deer and us is that we may decide that we can afford to sleep longer. If a deer does that, it may cost him his life. If you are going to survive and thrive in the wild, divergent thinking is a necessary survival skill. It should be instinct, your first nature, a strategy that gives you evolutionary advantage. This is why divergents, both natural and nurtured minds, can survive and thrive in any setting. The more they are exposed to life and different experiences, the more their knowledge base and capabilities grow and synthesize to achieve the flawless exercise of divergent thinking.

Picture being in the mind of divergents like William Shakespeare, Albert Einstein, Ralph Waldo Emerson, Katherine G. Johnson, Ellen Ochoa, Michelle Obama ... There is a reason why they can relate to music and the arts. In their thinking, they too live the "jazz" life. Divergents set the pace for the jazz combo with confidence and conviction in their baseline and improvisational skills, while the orchestra (the norm) plays the music of the system. What an amazing gift to be able to function between what is possible and what is impossible from the perspective of social norms. It may be one of the hardest things for you to do, because you may feel as though you don't fit anywhere. Rest assured, though, that you fit any and everywhere you want, if you see your way to it. You are not alone. Once you realize that, you're ready to start making things happen. Being different and thinking differently is a privilege not a burden. Make this the first day you think and live for possibilities. Remember, delayed is not denied. Some things in life take longer to manifest, and the birth of your divergent soul and your purpose just might. The finer things always take time to refine. To awaken them, you must put yourself out there by experiencing and challenging life. Employ patience, finesse, an abandoned approach, and even caution through divergent thinking. Figure out which requires what and master the art. Identify mentors, accountability partners, and align yourself with people heading in the same direction or who have been there, done that. Better to counsel with the wise than with fools. Surround yourself with those who fill in your knowledge gaps to make you stronger and wiser. There is no shame in doing so or in taking advice from others in the know. No one can know everything, but knowing a fair bit about a lot will serve you well. Don't miss your solo. Open your world to endless possibilities through divergent thinking! Win, lose, or draw, love the skin YOU'RE in!

Chapter 6

DEFINING PATHS: CONNECT THE DOTS

*"All the world's a stage,
And all the men and women merely players:
They have their exits, and their entrances;
And one man in his time plays many parts . . . "*

—William Shakespeare

Dear Society,

Fear is the thwarter of dreams. It plays tricks on us, hiding chances and causing us to fear a change in course. It's all in your mind. Take a leap of faith. Seize your chance. Fear has no power over you that you don't give it.

The fear to live disguises itself in many ways. The bottom line upfront is that it all begins and ends with you. You have the power to fuel it or to smother it. Once you make the choice of which ring to step into, commit and own the choice. If you don't take control of life, it will simply happen to you, leaving you discontent and with chronic depression, spinning in circles. Contrary to the unfortunate all too common belief held by so many, it's not impossible to define your own path no matter your situation or station in life. Divergent thinking will give you options and help you develop your strategy in short order and on the fly. All you need do is change your perspective. If you could imagine and believe in your heart that your station in life was meant to be the pressure, the fire to motivate and encourage you to emerge from it and lift others with you, what would you be capable of? It is time to leave the playground and put away childish things to begin walking in your adult purpose. You must define your own path to find fulfillment. It does not matter that you may not know how to go about doing so. Just start walking and connect the dots. You have the choice to be a victim or the victor.

The days of traditional thinking about making a lifelong career in one industry to achieve success are long gone. Don't be afraid of that. An unfortunate number of people ignore the fact that your reality can change with different stages of life. Then what? The reality has pitted those less and unprepared against those who can adapt to that fact. Today, it is not uncommon to switch career fields and diversify your portfolio of competencies. More and more employers actually view this as preferable for the value-add. Think about it . . . if the premise behind diversifying your financial portfolio has proven to provide a greater chance of sheltering you from certain risk, adverse loss, or total ruin, would it not stand to reason that diversifying your skill sets and experiences might provide a similar outcome in defining your career path and finding your purpose? The gift of life to human beings, aside from living it, is free will. However, the complexity of life begins to unfold with this gift. One choice leads to another, affects the other, and sets off a chain reaction of occurrences and consequences involving more than just you (Enter Fear center stage). The key is how you respond, and the trick is navigating it all. Quincy Roberts, philanthropist and CEO of Roberts Trucking, and I met at Indiana University School of Music. We were both pursuing degrees in music to become opera singers, travel the world, and move masses. Quincy had a brief career for several years working for opera companies and independently. Then he found himself at a crossroads. He recounts his transition from the world of opera to construction and trucking, two paths that couldn't be more different than he could've imagined but which led him to connect the next dot on the road to fulfillment and eventual purpose:

> Anytime you make a huge career change, it can be quite disturbing. You have to ask yourself, "Am I doing the right thing?" You have to look at your motivation for doing it. My grandparents started Roberts Trucking in 1979. Approaching retirement, they decided they wanted to keep the company in the family and offered me the opportunity. I decided to try my hand and see what it was about. I had an upcoming engagement, canceled it, and moved back to Dallas. I faced a lot of difficulties in gaining access to capital, ways in attracting customers, and so on. I started in 2006 and a year later the economic downturn came. I went into a business without a high demand at the time but saw it as a good thing. I learned a great deal and realized I had a knack for it. Now we've expanded from trucking to offering services in excavating, demolition, and trucking targeting heavy highway industry and public infrastructure projects (for example, airports, highways). I didn't come from a business background, even though as a singer you are technically working for yourself. I had not taken a business class and did not know what it took to run a successful business, but I learned. As a business

owner, I didn't have any experience, only the knowledge I had gained from my grandparents. I didn't know how to communicate with customers. So, everything I did from the initial side was, "Well, I am going to give it the old college try."

Plan as you might, plans will falter and life will require improvisation. Quincy was convinced his purpose lay awaiting him on the operatic stage. Little did he know. He adopted the mind-set of living the jazz life. It and divergent thinking informed his way and empowered his decision-making process to success and recognition by programs as the Ernst & Young Entrepreneur of the Year. In his early thirties, Quincy became one of the youngest CEOs in the country with one of the largest black-owned construction companies in the Dallas, Texas area employing upward of 250 persons.

If you are divergent by nature, these opportunities in life are merely exercises in creativity, challenges to a riddle by which you perfect your craft. Your perspective is already focused on you as the pacesetter. But what of those not exposed to the jazz life? If you are a planner and live your life by a plan, life will teach you that it has little concern or respect for your plan. It will require flexibility from you, or else its course can and will undo you. Make your plans and work through them, but set your plans up like a jazz chart. The outline is there, giving you some structure, but so is the opportunity for improvisation. Next, find your willpower, find your strength. The struggle is real, whether in your mind, heart, or circumstance. You have a choice and that choice is to conquer life with its obstacles or to allow life to conquer you. The choice for me has always been simple and one of my mantras, "Be a chain breaker and difference maker." You cannot expect anyone to hand anything to you, so you MUST move to action. Even if you are handed something, you still have action steps to take. Stop presenting your mind with excuses;

they build bridges to nowhere. Make a decision and tame your impulse to retreat. It is time to access that self-assertive, creative drive and start connecting the dots. If you do, doors will open and it will all start to make sense.

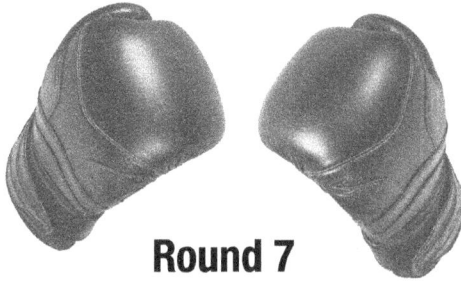

Round 7

Graduate School Challenges

My faith was immediately challenged, even before leaving Texas. Fortunately, that seed was planted in me as a child and I was prepared for the challenges. From having relationships to obtaining employment to juggling finances and playing catch-up academically, had it not been for my spiritual grounding and growing transformation, I would have mentally been out of the game. My network, inclusive of church family, sorority sisters, music fraternity family, staff, and students at the African American Arts Institute, and others with whom I connected and built healthy, uplifting relationships, kept me encouraged and focused.

I moved through my program with the excellence I had come to be known for; however, the performance side, which had come so easily and naturally for me in the past, became difficult. In an ironic way, my vocal challenges were a metaphor for life in that natural talent can only carry you so far. As with life, singing requires a foundation, and my training began late in life. I found myself discontent with my progress and considered abandoning my passion altogether.

About the same time, an opportunity presented itself through my old NPHC connection, Dr. Gordon. Following my final master's concert, he approached me with a proposition that would take me down a diverging path and further prepare me for things to come. I did not get caught up in the thought or fear of redirection, only in opportunity and service to a near and dear organization. I eagerly expressed my interest and set a meeting, with no thought as to how it would all fit together or how my life could change.

When I accepted the position, I was twenty-five years old. I started as an executive assistant, became assistant director within a year, and was appointed executive director the following year upon Dr. Gordon's retirement. I was the first female and the youngest executive director in the history of the organization. Working at NPHC headquarters was my first real trial run at divergent thinking, or at transferring knowledge and know-how across fields. I was surprised how naturally it came! Rebuilding the organization from the ground up, my creative side would allow me to come up with visions and overall plans; my analytical and detail-oriented side would take over for the research and particulars of the plans; they had both come back into play for the strategy; and the process would continue back and forth as one mind, like a well-oiled machine. I was operating as if I had an MBA and experience in business for years. It honestly kind of freaked me out. Who knew?! I would later discover that singers and musicians are uniquely suited to do just that— we are divergent by nature, studies, and craft.

Things started to hum at NPHC headquarters, so I decided to remain in Bloomington (my plan was three years and out) and start the doctoral program. Meanwhile, I was still challenged to find the right vocal technique (foundation), and once again found myself contemplating the role of my gift, when the opportunity to travel to Salzburg, Austria, and attend the Mozarteum presented itself. Without hesitation, I began the application process, with no clue as to how I would cover my expenses or manage my commitments back in the States. I felt a pull and simply moved to action; the rest worked itself out with creativity and favor. Austria was the next redefining and transformative time in my life. There, I encountered the incomparable Grace Bumbry, who took me under her wing after that summer as an apprentice, developing and grooming me—mentally, physically, vocally, and spiritually—in that order. I returned to the States after my hiatus a different person, eager to step into the ring and ready for my challengers.

Bloomington, Indiana was all about charting my course and preparing me holistically for my purpose. What I came to realize concerning faith is that so many people live based on the faith and spirituality of their parents and never truly find their own beliefs and relationship with God. For that experience, you must step into the ring with life to take on the challenge. You cannot have a testimony without a test, and to walk in your purpose requires tests. Bernice Johnson Reagon rightly said, "Life's challenges are not supposed to paralyze you, they're supposed to help you discover who you are." Salzburg helped me discover who I was. Sometimes you must go to grow. To develop personally, professionally, and spiritually, exposure to new and different things and people is a requirement. We get too comfortable not only where we are but also with what and who we know. If these things are not changing and growing with you, they are likely holding you back from your potential. Make some moves! If you are not undergoing some sort of progression, you are not walking in purpose but instead merely existing. If your system can only handle small, go small. But go! If you have some tolerance for risk and nothing to lose but your codependency, GO BIG and don't look back. Your successful outcome depends on it. Whatever it takes, go to grow! Instead of fearing change, embrace it. Learn to adapt to your environment quickly. Figure out how to survive and thrive while in it. Life can deal punishing blows. You just have to figure out when to duck, bob, and weave. "Courage is not the absence of fear, but rather the judgment that something else is more important than fear" (Ambrose Redmoon). You are that something else. You are more important.

Life experiences, how we think, and the paths we choose play important roles. In the boxing ring of life, we encounter old nemeses and new opponents. You will sometimes have the upper hand but mostly not. Your response as the underdog will either stifle you and cause your knees to buckle or propel you forward to victory. Opportunities present themselves and direct our path. It's on us to exhibit patience, to recognize, and to choose to take them even without knowing where they may ultimately lead. As you move through life, employ your divergent thinking toolkit and begin to connect the dots. Remember, you are the pacesetter, the conductor. View life as your jazz combo, your orchestra. Focus on solutions, not the problem. It does nothing for morale or motivation to dwell on the problem. You may not see the way forward completely clearly, but simply moving toward your goal will summon the Law of Attraction. Just keep moving and focusing forward. The only thing that looking back can do for you is trip you up. Your confusion or discontentment is just a temporary response to a momentary challenge. If you're not where you want to be in life, consider your options and how they fit with your skill sets—not your major, not your position but your capabilities. Lay out the puzzle and find the connecting pieces. If that opportunity fits into your now and the door is open, go with it. Don't overthink it. Recalibrate later. Just keep connecting the dots with a little imagination. Don't argue for perceived limitations. Move to action, and your decisiveness will overcome doubt and fear every time to liberate and empower you. You are not in competition with anyone but yourself. Meet your challenges as they come.

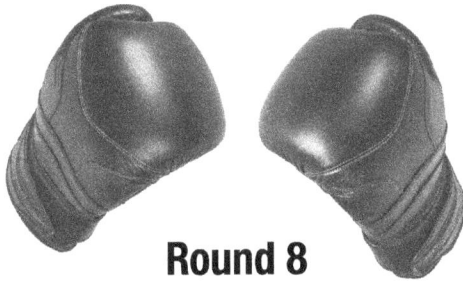

Round 8
Young Professional Riding High

I returned to my position with NPHC and resumed my studies. I was tuned into my channel without white noise or static of any kind. Simultaneously, I successfully moved through my doctoral program, built partnerships across industries and traveled the world, and served as a caregiver to my father, whom I reconnected with just down the road settled in Louisville, Kentucky after his retirement from horse racing. The balancing act was real. No time for a social life but absolutely no regrets. NPHC was my training ground and means by which I filled over half of my toolkit for success. My musical training provided the presence, creativity, innovation, analytics, and collaborative spirit, among other transferable skills and assets to the package. I had stepped into the professional ring with an impressive record of knockouts. I remained with the organization another four years, until managing my reality began to take a toll on my health. I made the tough decision to resign from the National Pan-Hellenic Council.

Leaving NPHC left me with another exercise in divergent thinking to connect the next dot. The headquarters was located on the campus of Indiana University and situated as an auxiliary organization, so I was familiar with campus life, systems, and the administration. As mentioned, I had also taken a few classes in higher education administration at SWT, so looking to the university for employment was logical. After an interview for another position, a search committee member reached out and presented me with another option. It was a no-brainer. It fully met my checklist and was a much better fit with growth potential. As had been my modus operandi, I worked my way up quickly in two years to three different positions, with the third ultimately being the director's seat of the Indiana University Bloomington Hudson and Holland Scholars Program (HHSP). It was in serving the extraordinary students of HHSP that I discovered my passion and talent for helping define the paths of others academically, personally, and professionally. I brought the same work ethic and holistic ideologies that I had drawn on in previous positions to HHSP, finding synergies and building partnerships on campus and externally across industries for program support, student access, development, and placement. After five years of successfully transforming the Program into the only holistic development scholarship program of its kind in the country, I found myself with a monumental decision to step away to protect the 600+ students of the Program and what we had built. Converging circumstances provided clear guidance that I had fulfilled my purpose there and that it was time to move on. My decision was not taken without a great deal of consideration and angst; however, being in the ring with life had taught me that when it was time, it was time to call a draw. To connect the next dots that needed to be connected, not only for me but for all involved, I had to make room. In the process, my entrepreneurial spirit was calling.

Times are changing. It's now on us to figure out how to operate in a dynamic environment. When it is time to move on, it's time to move on. Develop, diversify your skill sets, and network, and you will always have employment options. You can no longer rely on traditional education or training models. Conventional wisdom (generally accepted theories or beliefs) may help you outline your path and get your foot in the door, but it will not keep you there nor help you define it. The concept of defining paths is an organic and creative process with a blueprint assumption that will help you navigate. Everything in your life has a purpose. While multiple pieces may seem not to fit, your goal is to find the similarities and connect the dots. Doing so requires operating without a box and trusting in something bigger and higher than you. It's about turning your weaknesses into strengths one day at a time, one dot at a time. So, when you are weak, say you're strong. While there's strategy in faking it until you make it, once your foot is in the door a measure of competency can only carry you so far. Don't expect promotion just because you show up every day. You get out of something what you put in. Become a master of that subject and become invaluable. Don't be afraid to walk the outer limits and try new things. Gain new perspective. From it will come validation and empowerment to believe in yourself. Continue walking your path and making forward motion to achieve your personal measure of success. It's never too late! Stop that nonsensical, debilitating chatter in your head. You can run and hide, or stand up and get in the ring. Even though things may not have worked out the way you envisioned, that only means you have the opportunity for a new vision. Your aptitude is largely determined by your attitude, which controls your altitude! Reality is what you make it. Define your own path, and don't concern yourself with the road not taken. The road less traveled by will make all the difference.

My life has been led by making lemonade out of lemons and sweetening it to my taste through the natural marriage of engaging in divergent thinking and defining my path. Don't let others make up your mind or control your outlook. If something is worth fighting for, stand and fight. You are worth fighting for! Fight to define your path. When you do so, you will find your purpose. You are not here by happenstance. You were not a mistake. Don't let anyone put into your head the idea that you are. Love yourself enough to believe in yourself and find out why you were put here on earth. It was for a reason. Place faith in your Higher Power, not in man, and keep walking it out. No one and no situation can stop you from fulfilling your purpose if your mind, heart, and spirit are right. Be resilient, be encouraged, be blessed, and live your life without fear. What happens will happen. That is the gift and complexity of human choice. Stop worrying about the bout. Get in the ring and win the fight. Work hard in silence and let your success be the noise. Everything has a time and a season, including levels and stages of success. We don't always get our due from man, but trust that your work is not in vain. Always put your best foot forward with a smile on your face. Trust that favor will find you when it is time for your elevation. If you are performing your work with a work ethic beyond reproach and your motives are pure, promotion will come. Persevere, keep your eyes on the prize, and keep jealousy and envy from your heart regarding the accomplishments of others. Find and create passion in what you do, put yourself in the right frame of mind, and the right people will notice.

My mother often reminds me, "If God leads you to it, He will take you through it." A worthy and tested mantra, it has sustained, kept, and blessed me. It speaks to the power of having an active, living spiritual source in your life, a power outside yourself that can magnify your ability to see and connect the dots. If you want to be empowered and take your life to the next level, tap into the spirit. It will not only change your heart and mind but also give you supernatural strength and focus. Your limits will be the ones you set. Only you can hold you back by limiting your exposure to what and who is known to you. Challenge your assumptions to grow and equip yourself. Make room in your life for something and someone new and different. Your story is not yet written. Don't let others determine your path or write it. The only author who can do you justice is you. Defining your path requires extraordinary resilience and a willingness to travel it. There's a reason you are where you are. Figure it out and proceed accordingly. Want a hint? You're either there to breathe life into something, to uplift others, or to be a stepping stone to your elevation, which will encompass both. The interesting thing about defining your path is that while it is about you, it is not about you.

Once you've had a chance to grow, learn, synthesize, and process, you are ready to apply that knowledge across domains (divergent thinking). You're ready to define your path. Your confidence and perspective on your capabilities will change. Make sure you constantly check and address your underlying mind-set. Mind-set affects performance. You have complete control to change that. Put yourself in the driver's seat and don't be afraid to walk the outer limits. Think and see apart from the norm. That river you could never cross, that wall you could never get over, that mountain you've been trying to move, you will find a way over, under, around, or through. There's always an answer when you leverage the power of divergent thinking. Don't worry about what others are doing or the path they are on. When naysayers question or ridicule you, always take the higher ground. "When they go low, we go high" (Michelle Obama). Your time is coming. When you are true to yourself, you cannot make a wrong step. Love the skin YOU'RE in!

Chapter 7

DANCING IN THE RING: THE BALANCING ACT

"Balance is not something you find, it's something you create."

—Jana Kingsford

Dear Society,

The act of balancing is an elusive endeavor. Instead, manage your reality. Seek right proportions that will allow you to steady yourself in the ring of life. Stay light on your feet and don't allow the pressure of the ring to weigh you down. Self-awareness, development, and mind-set are key. Keep dancing and you will fall into rhythm.

The act of balancing is an elusive endeavor. In all honesty, there is no such thing as balance in a dynamic human life, only shifts in time, energy, focus, and scope of priority. The term itself gives a misleading impression of reality. Instead, change your perception and seek right proportions that will allow you to manage and steady yourself in the ring of life. Creating the illusion of balance requires recognition, a combination of skills, conscious effort, and adjustments as needed. The power to do so comes from the mind, and how you use it determines your success. Stay light on your feet and dance around the pressures of life as you manage your reality. Strive for excellence and realize perfection is unattainable. The thought that it is attainable is either a self-inflicted performance anxiety or the result of a life trauma. Release that hurt, hang-up, or habit. Don't set yourself up. Get your mind and spirit right, and the rest will follow. Then you will be able to make positive, productive life-giving choices.

Just think, if we all prioritized and concentrated our energy, focus, and time on this earth to be instruments of love and peace, truly what a world this would be. "Lord, make me an instrument of your peace; where there is hatred, let me sow love; when there is injury, pardon; where there is doubt, faith; where there is despair, hope; where there is darkness, light; and where there is sadness, joy." Can you imagine the state of our health and relationships? The fact of the matter is that Saint Francis asks a great deal of mere mortals in this prayer . . . or does he? The subconscious mind takes you where you want to go. If you believe something in your heart and spirit, you will manifest that thing. But let's start by applying this concept of love and peace on an individual level. Internal conflict and a lack of self-love are their antagonists. Without the know-how and discipline to manage time, energy, and focus, you have less chance to successfully function at optimal capacity in tuning into your channel, employing divergent thinking, and defining your path. The scope of priority is easier: you simply decide, commit, and do it.

A boxer doesn't enter a ring without training and developing the skill of boxing. Without doing so, that boxer's expectation of winning is slim to none and will likely lead to a loss. Dancing is your art, your skill, so you should do likewise. Train and develop your technique. The win will go to the most prepared. Rodolfo Menjivar, author of *Life Balance*, stresses the importance of personal development through focusing on mental, physical, emotional, and spiritual health as key to the balancing act in finding and strengthening yourself as well as discovering your mission and purpose in life. He goes on to further suggest that finding "balance" applies to every aspect of life, to both internal and external elements. To achieve this stability while dancing in the ring with life, focus on engaging spar partners who will help you develop recognition and combination skills to manage your reality and build your confidence:

1. Mind-set and Emotions

You are uniquely and divinely made. Know that and understand what it means. You are not a mistake, and nothing about you is an accident. Don't let life or others into your head who might cause you to believe otherwise. Find those things that ground you in reality. Keep your emotions balanced to maintain a clear head. Showing emotion is not a bad thing, but adopt the practice of keeping all things in moderation, understanding that it is impossible always to do so but that it should be the goal. This philosophy is conveyed in the Divergent Series: Allegiant through the assertion that if you are too brave, you risk cruelty; too peaceful, passivity; and too smart, a lack of compassion.

Take time to really look at your life and consider how you're feeling and your state of mind. Work on your hurts, hang-ups, and habits. Nothing and no one is worth derailing your peace and sanity. Maintain that perspective. Mind-set and emotions should have the highest place in your scope of priorities. The lower they are, the higher your chance at failing to conquer life.

2. Education

Educate yourself and be a lifelong learner so that you may free yourself from social conditioning and other control mechanisms. Develop your knowledge and know-how, whether through formal education, vocational training programs, or self-study. Then find opportunities to engage in application of what you've learned. Think about and internalize your findings so that you can retrieve them at will and when necessary. Personal and professional development is paramount in the facilitation of divergent thinking and defining paths. Education is the key that unlocks those opportunities.

3. Healthy Relationships

Pay every attention to what is going on inside your mind and your heart. When either or both are unhealthy, you are unhealthy and may potentially face trouble for making bad decisions concerning relationships—familial, platonic, or otherwise. When you have heart health, you can give and receive love; therefore, you will know when it is not received or reciprocated. Healthy relationships are important support systems and safe havens. Fulfill your responsibilities to them, but set and keep healthy boundaries and do not maintain impenetrable walls.

4. Work

Work is tricky. It is one of our most socially conditioned environments and an indispensable function of life for most of us. When you have a high-performance standard and work ethic for yourself, the difficulty comes in adapting the former and understanding that not everyone has the latter. Simultaneously, you must work to reconcile management culture.

As in life itself, work environments will show you what you're made of and present you with worthy opponents when you least expect it, so expect the unexpected. One of the most compromising challenges is ethical decision-making. The ethics of a work environment can test your faith and the essence of who you are. The combo punches that are thrown may wear on you and can lead down a slippery slope. Be wary of jumping on the bandwagon based on empty promises and moral degradation, or even of choosing the "safe" route and going along to get along (which most people do). You must sleep at night and live with your choices. Everyone else is not you, so do what you must do. Stand your ground. Whether you realize it or not, every time you compromise your moral values, you lose a piece of yourself and your connection to humanity. Even though the game may be rigged and the playing field uneven, you don't have to be like everyone else. Be better. People-pleasing leads down a destructive path. You will have to choose, and the right choices are usually the most unpopular.

Only you can account for your decisions, actions, and behaviors. No one made you do something, and no one can sell you short but you. What are YOU about? What do YOU stand for? Compromise where you can, but where you can't, don't. When it comes to your character and integrity, compromise should have no place. Even if everyone is telling you that something wrong is right, your heart will tell you the truth, if it is healthy. To come out the other side a conqueror, you must have the heart and stance of a warrior in order to make the complex and hard decisions. While we cannot control what happens to us, we can control how we react to circumstances and the choices we make as a result to manage our reality.

5. Extracurricular Activities

We should all enjoy some aspect of social experience and fun. Focus your time and energy on extracurricular activities, that is, things that address, protect, and challenge your mental, physical, and spiritual health. These are your pillars of strength and cornerstones. You cannot involve yourself in everything, so be mindful not to overdo it. When your body indicates rest, listen.

6. Accountability

Accountability is the measure of a person. In all that you do, be accountable. Acknowledge and live up to your responsibilities and commitments. Be honest with yourself and assess the areas of your life that present themselves to you as opponents in this area. It's never too late to address them. Learn to say "no" before you reach your limits or if you are incapable of doing something or being something to someone else. Your word is your bond and, once broken, is difficult to recover.

7. Drive

Drive comes from intrinsic motivation or circumstance. If it comes from circumstance, you must program the behavior into your subconscious. Remember, captain and crew. Drive will yield energy, initiative, determination, and ambition to find and walk in your purpose. Drive will grow your confidence and help you step into your power to claim what's yours. It will give you the ability to keep moving forward.

8. Reflection and Examination

Take time to reflect upon and examine where you are in life. Conduct regular self-assessments. You may find that you are missing out on the experience of truly living because you're afraid to dance in the ring for fear of inability or failure. In that checkup, make sure you are not speaking self-fulfilling prophecies of negativity or sabotage into your mind-set. Reflection and examination will help you tune into your channel and manage anxieties, doubts, and fears if you are honest with yourself; avoid the plague of denial. Deliberate on, accept, and put solutions to your findings into motion.

9. Live

Why are we here? What is our purpose? Life is worth living and discovering the answers. Rediscover yourself or get to know yourself for the first time. You're going to encounter resistance. That's a given. Make up your mind to be happy and then be happy. See the big picture while moving among the detail and keep your eyes on that prize. Stop worrying about disappointing others and live your life. While trying to find individuality within a family unit or the human collective under societal pressures is more than challenging, it is not impossible. Keep a positive outlook. If those around you love, support, and respect you, they will encourage and uplift you. They will manage reality with you. If not, this will be telling. Do not compromise your dreams and happiness; life choices don't have to be an either/or. When you set your goals, be flexible in executing them and accepting the outcomes. Life is unpredictable. But if prepared, you can enjoy the ride and conquer. "Open up your mind and just be willing to listen because when you start listening, then you'll start understanding. When you start understanding, that journey will guide you to where you need to be" (Kristy Morrison). Feel the beat of the ring and learn to dance.

10. Empower and Connect

Empower yourself by accepting the challenge of life and learning to manage your reality. Connect with others. Build your network and relationships with people who have lived and are living a similar story with similar management requirements to help you gain insight as well as give you support and motivation. Don't be afraid to ask for or take advice, but realize that what works for one person may not work for another, so find the right mix for you. Share your experiences and learn to accept constructive criticism. However, be mindful to allow only fruit-bearing individuals to speak light into your life. Wisdom begets wisdom. Once you discriminate the foolish from the wise, listen more than you speak. When you do speak, you will have something to say. You will be and feel empowered ready to accept and embrace life's challenges.

When managing your reality, strive for excellence. Realize that the expectation and goal of perfection is unattainable. The thought that it is either, is self-inflicted performance anxiety or the result of life trauma. Release that hurt, hang-up, or habit. Don't set yourself up for disappointment. An extreme in anything can be detrimental. Managing your reality means that you have a handle on the various elements in your life and that your mind and heart are not being pulled disproportionately in one direction or the other. It requires grit. Approach the endeavor with the understanding that it takes time and effort to overcome habitual patterns and create new ones. It may not look pretty while you are in the midst of things, but you can keep after it. The distractions of life may keep you on your heels, so consciously make time to exercise and develop a holistic regimen in your daily life and solidify it into your state of being. Put into practice techniques to control your enemies. Most foe are bred from fear, and we know that fear breeds fear. Fear of something that is impending can inhibit the mind and paralyze the body and spirit. When an aspect of your life has the potential to introduce fear, seize the upper hand by controlling the response of your heart and mind. Stay out of the corner. The freer you feel, the more composed you will remain. Commit to cleaning house for at least ninety consecutive days and check your progress. How you train and practice for life's bouts will determine your outcome.

If you are broken in mind, you will be broken in spirit, which will leave the body defenseless. Finding your faith and walking in it gives you access to supernatural strength to fully access and coordinate mind, body, and spirit. When you learn to manage your reality, you will be able to gain and keep your peace and perspective. Keep moving forward. Remind yourself why you're doing what you're doing. If you cannot come up with a rationale or justification for why you're doing something, perhaps that is a clue you shouldn't be doing it. "Don't waste your love. energy and time" (Susan Buffett). Stay out of denial and acknowledge when your internal or external equilibrium is off. You can't do and be everything for everybody, so don't tax your mind or body with that standard or expectation.

To move to the next level, dance in the ring, and conquer life, you will need to fortify yourself with additional tools including discipline, strength, a healthy amount of fear for discernment, respect for your opponent, and respect for higher purpose. Adopt the principle of holism. Holistic living rounds out an individual. Have the drive and determination of an athlete, the creativity and finesse of an artist, and for good measure, dignity, graciousness, and humility. Become and remain self-aware. It is empowering and will allow you to manage your reality in the midst of the storm. Love the skin YOU'RE in!

Chapter 8

STEPPING INTO THE RING: LOVE, LOSS, HEARTACHE, AND HEARTBREAK

"People come into your life for a reason, a season or a lifetime. When you figure out which one it is, you will know what to do for each . . . "

—Unknown

Dear Society,

Love is life. Love is what heals. Love is what holds. Love is what binds. Love is what provides clear perspective. When you have a heart condition, based on a lack of love or on self-pity for yourself, you're on the way to flatlining. Improve your heart health by dealing with and getting over your hurts, hang-ups, and habits. Keep your pulse strong and steady.

The greatest challenge in life is loving yourself enough to discover who you are, apart from others. The second greatest is being happy with what you find. We often busy ourselves and put up appearances to mask our hurt. Hurt and insecure people find fault and lash out for a reason; life can harden you. Yet the issues do not reside outside with others but within us. To keep your pulse strong and steady and to ensure your heart health, acknowledge your pain. Do the work on the front end, particularly before you involve others. Sometimes we think we have done the work, and possibly we have to a degree; however, unless you have uncovered and faced all your demons, you've not invested enough in your holistic healing to step into the ring and conquer them. Denial can make you believe otherwise. Self-justification is a powerful force that provides temporary cover, clouds the mind, and prevents good judgment, but it cannot cover a heart condition.

Our emotional being and choices come directly from the heart. According to Thomas Merton, the Trappist monk and author of the best-selling autobiography *The Seven Storey Mountain* (1948):

> We cannot be happy if we expect to live all the time at the highest peak of intensity. Happiness is not a matter of intensity but of balance and order and rhythm and harmony. Music is pleasing not only because of the sound but because of the silence that is in it: without the alternation of sound and silence there would be no rhythm.

These same words from *Seven Storey Mountain* appear in the chapter called "Being and Doing" in Merton's collection of essays *No Man Is an Island* (1955), titled after the poet and priest John Donne's concept of the interconnectedness of human lives. While the words speak to the intensities in life and the complementary nature of dualities—sound and silence, love and loss—they further speak to the fact that nothing and no one comes from or exists for the sake of self. Everything is connected. So, it stands to reason that if we are doing more than just being, we can and will be influenced by both internal and external forces. The important thing is not to let them derail you. Happiness comes from our ability to regulate the intensity of both our internal emotions and external influences while continuing to live. If you've done the work, you don't have to be afraid to live and let people in. Prioritize your heart health by managing your reality. Accept the circle of life, keep your perspective looking forward, find your rhythm, and maintain harmony. Then you will be able to control your responses to life.

Once you have decided to discover the true you, you are stepping into the ring with life, and life is unpredictable. All you can do is proactively manage it and your happiness. In addition to battling regularly occurring societal pressures, the heartache and heartbreak of losing loved ones and relationships can throw you into a tailspin and literally break you. Events of this nature throw off our equilibrium. Our emotions are compromised, in turn jeopardizing our mind-set and choices. Those individuals who are more prepared will be fortunate to tread water until they are ready to swim again. Those who are less prepared will find themselves moving backward instead of forward. They say time heals all wounds. I have found that it does, when you let it. The length of time it takes is up to you. The difficult choice is to accept the loss and move on. No matter your tolerance for risk in living, life will not come without love, loss, heartache, and heartbreak, but it will not break you. These opponents serve to train us and make us stronger. Commit to living your life with that perspective while walking your path of discovery.

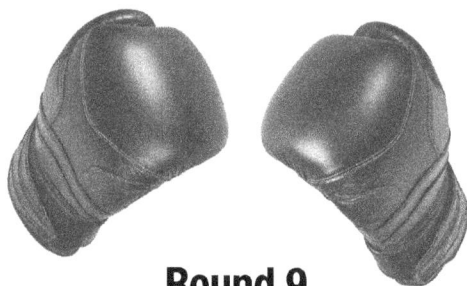

Round 9

Family Circles

As mentioned, my path led me full circle to find my biological father in Louisville, Kentucky. My parents had divorced when I was fifteen years old. It was almost surreal to learn that he was only two hours away from me. The knowledge brought back all kinds of feelings and emotions that rushed to the surface. While I felt curious, I hardened my heart toward the thought of seeing him. I sat on the information until the Lord started to deal with me. Sunday after Sunday, I sat in church thinking about my father, trying to maintain my anger and self-righteousness (I didn't realize it was that at the time). The funny thing about that is, when you are sincerely seeking spiritual growth, a pure heart, and a relationship with God, you cannot harden your heart toward another. You will be convicted and led to reassess yourself, as well as caused to look at their heart, understand their plight, and forgive. Light cannot reside with darkness, and light will always win. Over the next several months, the light inside started to transform my heart and soften it more and more toward reaching out to my father. I finally made the call after finding myself face down on the church floor sobbing uncontrollably because I let go of the hurt and anger I was carrying all those years. I was ready to start healing.

My roommate and sister from another mother offered to travel to Louisville with me. She was a godsend. When life brought my dad and me back together, it was as if we had never been apart. Granted, I proceeded with caution, but the walls were penetrable. I learned so much on that Saturday and gained a new perspective on my relationship with my dad that I had not even considered would be possible. While I was wearing my pain all those years, so was he. I came to realize that day that my father was human and fallible, but that I was always in his heart and on his mind. Before I departed, he shared a profound request he had made of God while surviving cancer and that was to spare his life until he saw me once more. You can imagine . . . I was done after that. Hearing my father speak those words floored me. On that side of the family, saying "I love you" or anything equating to that was uncommon. We somehow knew it and had each other's back, but those words were never spoken. That request was honored, and we were given the opportunity to rebuild our relationship and rediscover each other after a decade and before his homegoing.

I had the opportunity to rediscover my father and myself through both of our eyes. I remember dancing with him at his birthday party and watching those little chicken legs move so fast to zydeco that it made my head spin, then slowing things down for a father-daughter dance to Luther Vandross's "Dance with My Father." See, I had been in denial for years believing I was indifferent to his absence. My stepfather, whom I adored and loved as a father, had managed to fill most of a gigantic hole inside me, which allowed me to simply kick dirt over the rest. That day, during that dance, I felt a joy and comfort I had not felt since childhood. The smile on my father's face and the sheer happiness emanating from his heart were real and a resuscitating jolt to mine. I realized the time I had wasted and the destructive choices I had made in my personal life because I had subconsciously prioritized my hurt and directed my energy toward it. Guarding that hurt had done nothing but hurt me and wasted time . . . precious time . . .

Dad was tough and scrappy for his size and stature. He had a gentle and pure heart and would give the shirt off his back to a stranger. His personality was magnetic, and everyone loved him. As he loved to remind family and friends, "I'm nationwiiiiiide . . . " and it was the truth. Nevertheless, his challenges were constant and kept him in the ring. After battling cancer and conquering it like a champ, he began to suffer dementia and complications as well as other health issues that could not be successfully treated. As his condition worsened and he had a few major health scares, we made the call together to relocate him to Bloomington, where I became his caregiver and provided him a better quality of life until his passing a few years later.

I simultaneously threw myself into plans for his homegoing, reconnecting with that side of my family, and also planning a summer study program for my students to Ghana. Before I knew it, almost three years had passed and I had not properly mourned my father. My solution was not to process my emotions but to bury them with busyness until I was introduced to Celebrate Recovery at the City Church For All Nations (CCFAN). I recall seeing the advertisement several Sundays during the Welcome and my interest being piqued, but something was holding me back—pride. But the seed had been planted; I just needed a little water to start the growth process. Driving home from work one day, I had every intention of heading home but found myself in the church parking lot. When I came to CR, I had more than issues. I had subscriptions and didn't realize it. The majority of them stemmed from my relationship with my father. Yes, I had opened my heart and we had reconnected, but I had not done the real work of self-discovery, reconciliation, and healing within. I had so many hurts, hang-ups, and habits to work through that I went through the program twice!

Celebrate Recovery gave me the final tools for my toolkit to conquer life. After getting over my pride and initial uneasiness at listening to others and sharing, I was empowered and motivated to share at every meeting, particularly seeing the changes in my life that occurred with the application of the program's principles. What strikes me in accepting the circle of life is that had I not lost my father, I likely would not have arrived at self-love. I would not be who I am today. The journey of loving and losing led me to the ability to forgive and to the discovery of my true self. I imagine these are some of the greatest gifts a parent could give in their lifetime or posthumously.

What are the takeaways? The circle of life will always be that—a circle. Paths cross again and again. When life removes something, it gives something in return. Your heart can be mended, the holes can be filled, and the heart can heal. It all starts with learning to love yourself, which involves forgiving yourself for holding on to whatever thoughts or feelings you were harboring. Only then will you be able to forgive and love others. Punishment is a teaching mechanism for children. Trying to punish a loved one through mental or emotional abuse for something you perceived them doing to you, makes you no better and reveals your brokenness. Learn to forgive so that you may let go literally and figuratively. The struggle to hold on to the past may be weighing you down in ways you cannot even comprehend. Understand that you can't outrun or avoid life. Tragedy, loss is a part of it. You must find a way to accept it and move on. Bad things will not stop happening, but neither will the good. Once you accept these facts of life, you can truly run free. The good and the bad make us who we are. It's the yin and yang of life, and it shapes us.

Make sure the source code that shapes your reality is not skewed, meaning you've not created an alternate reality, nor are you operating on a system glitch. There is no time for this insanity. Holding on to anger and negativity creates that glitch, the loop of repeating the same actions, making the same choices and expecting different results. It gets you nowhere. Learn to live above your demons. Protect your mind and subject your thoughts to the positive. Everyone has a past as well as hurts which affect their choices. Perspective is everything. When we allow ourselves to exist and operate in an alternate reality and/or negativity, the truth is slanted and our perspective off. We justify our actions and prove our correctness through our own playbook of alternative facts by adjusting conversations and experiences so that they reconcile with what we see in our mind's eye. Why do we do this? Most people can't handle the truth of their choices or face their demons, so they create illusions or delusions to balance their state of mind and being. For these individuals, their perspective says that they've been wronged and had no part in the situation that they find themselves in. However, this perspective will lead to your undoing and down the path to insanity, if unchecked.

Self-pity comes in all forms. Whatever the form, it is a distraction and offers neither comfort nor a solution. Why waste time lamenting over your shortcomings or those of others? Self-pity is a costly indulgence and an excuse to avoid stepping into the ring with life. Guard your heart with love and honesty. They bring clarity and will protect your mind and keep your ways stable. Perspective can be your best friend or your worst enemy. Deal with your hurts, hang-ups, and habits so that you may celebrate your recovery. Appreciate and live every day. We were never promised life would be easy, but we were given the gift of choice. Meet your life challenges head-on. You're stronger than you know.

Round 10

Romance Pains and Gains

Jake was the unexpected love of my life, and I believed he would be that for a lifetime. He was my opposite and my equal. We complemented each other in every way. On paper, we were phenomenal. In real life, we were extraordinary. Together, we were a force, adventurous and ambitious. The relationship was natural, easy, and vibrant. The mutual love and support was there from the beginning. We were the envy of others and the model couple in mind, body, and spirit. Everyone thought we were in for the long haul. Our separation shocked both of us and those closest to us. But it was inevitable.

So, what happened? Our codependency and struggle to find and maintain our individuality were our undoing. Individuality cannot be found while in a relationship. You must enter a relationship with it. Managing a reality where one has not had the opportunity to know one's individuality and the other has is a powder keg waiting to be lit. When you know and understand that potential dynamic and respect it before entering a relationship, you have a legitimate hope that it will last a lifetime. First, find out who you are, what your limits are, and what you can and cannot live with or without before involving someone else. Know your goals, seek purpose, and communicate those things to that potential partner openly. Romantic relationships are not meant to merely live for someone else's happiness. You must live for yours, or you will find yourself unhappy.

Jake and I met at the tail end of difficult transitions we were making to the East Coast for different reasons for each of us. It was easy to find and take comfort in each other, particularly because of all the commonalities and the chemistry between us. We also made a pretty cute couple! Jake was a gentleman, cultured and refined unlike anyone I had experienced but had always imagined. At the same time, he could relate to anyone and fit in anywhere. He had an uncanny ability to adapt. It was easy to fall for him. After God, he was my rock, my support, and my biggest fan. He rescued me from the verge of despair and made me feel like a million bucks! He was my fairy-tale prince. Only problem, we weren't in a fairy tale. Time passed and we were extremely happy, until one day we weren't. We found ourselves in power struggles seeking space, identity, and purpose, not to mention combating forces outside of our relationship at work and in life in general. Our communication became stunted and with it the divide grew. We sought spiritual counseling for months, and things got better but fluctuated between great, good, and bad. Don't get me wrong, most of our time together was like a fairy tale, but it always felt like someone else's life. It was not until almost a year after our relationship ended that I processed my part in things and his role in my life.

They say opposites attract, but not opposites in different places in their life. While we thought that we were in a similar place, the things we each needed to recover from affected us in different ways, requiring different responses. We were both dealing with post-traumatic stress from our respective situations. Rushing into a committed relationship was not the answer. Being big on accountability, I sought to make amends after coming to this realization. I owned up to my part, apologized to him for my weakness, and thanked him for changing my life for the better by being in it. In my mind, I should've been strong enough to patiently wait and trust in the Lord and the capabilities I have been blessed with to pull me from despair and disappointment. But I am human and that is not the choice I made. Nonetheless, it was a choice that enriched my life and taught me invaluable lessons. I learned a major lesson that rushing life is not a wise choice. Relationships are a fragile thing. We initiate them with the best intentions, but we must allow them to happen organically. So, we must give each other the space and time we need; it's different for everyone. Then we can come together in commitment. Don't fear losing out on love because of time. Depending on how you use it, time can be your opponent or it can be your cornerman. I cannot say it enough . . . how you look at things—perspective—is everything. It will stabilize your mind-set, help you tune into your channel, and give you peace to be confident in and make healthy choices.

There is no bitterness in my heart. I forgave Jake almost immediately for his part in ending our relationship. Honestly, I believe we both saw it coming; however, we tried to hold on for whatever reason. I cannot speak for him, but I was trying to turn a reason and a season into a lifetime, instead of trusting the old saying "If you love something, set it free. If it comes back to you, it is yours. If it doesn't, it never was." So much wisdom and so much truth in that. When I reached out to Jake and thanked him for the time we shared, I was surprised by the emotion that flooded into my heart. It was no longer full of heartache or heartbreak but of love and joy for the revelation and release. I would not be who I am today had our paths not crossed. He was my earthly angel whom my God assigned when I needed him most. He helped propel me forward when I was ready to give up. Without Jake, I would have strayed from my path and missed my purpose. I am stronger, wiser, and so much better for Jake and what he brought to my life. I was his divine assignment and he mine. How did I heal? I let go. I let go of fear and chose strength. I let go of loss and chose to be happy. I let go and chose to live.

The loss of a parent is traumatic, but so is the loss of someone you believed you would spend the rest of your life with. The pain is real and is nothing to ignore. Don't bury your feelings. Mourn the loss and give your heart time to heal. Otherwise, you're more susceptible to falling victim to unwise choices and the fallout. Warren Buffett laments in the documentary about him, entitled *Becoming Warren Buffett*, "Love is a strange thing. You give it out, you get a whole bunch back. You hold onto it, you lose it." Relationships can change in the blink of an eye. The loss of love leads to heartache and heartbreak and can take you there, not only to unhappiness and tears but also to anger, blame, hopelessness, and depression. Rarely are the first reactions peace and inward reflection, but they are the most essential to preserving your heart health. Why is that? In an ironic way, the others are like comfort food. They are the most familiar, the easiest to come by. Most people have been socialized to respond in such ways. Whatever the case, your response is your response. The test is what you do after that. Let go, grieve, forgive, learn the lessons, then get back on your feet. Life happens and sometimes you lose the round. Good news! You can still win the match, so long as you keep your name on the fight card. Hearts heal and scars fade. Draw on the source of your strength. For me, that source is the Holy Spirit in me (Greater is He that is in me!).

Everyone has moments of weakness and makes compromising choices. Don't beat yourself up; you are human. What's important is that you can hear the voice of sanity calling and recover. Hopefully, it will not be too late. But if it is, move on. You don't have to force anything if it's meant for you. Maintain your individuality. If you are reacting based on someone else's emotional state, mood, or behavior, don't do that. Check yourself before it becomes habit. You can identify with your partner, but do not lose your identity. You are supposed to support, compliment, and counter the other when needed. Love yourself and your significant other enough to regulate your choices and actions. Relationships are tricky to navigate. While love can bind, it can also cause you to lose sight of who you are or compromise your standards. Sometimes what looks good on paper doesn't work in real life, no matter how much chemistry there is between two people. When two people are not meant to be together, the result will always be heartache and heartbreak. Hanging on, to simply hang on is prolonging the inevitable. Love the other person enough to wish them well and let them go. If you have yourself together (be honest) and question your partner's feelings toward you, there's a problem. Do not fear change or waste time and energy second-guessing your choices. Have a conversation face to face. You will know in your heart what you need to do. While the prospect of leaving the relationship may be a scary thing for you, view it as an opportunity for another chance and the start of your new life. Make the move. Have no regret and do not dwell on things. The past is the past. The only direction in life that matters is forward, never backward. There's no good and no purpose in looking back. Should've, would've, could've will set you up for the knockout. Bottom line, you cannot succeed while failing.

People stay in lopsided, dysfunctional romances all the time for fear of being alone, convincing themselves that they and their partner feel the same way about each other. They persuade themselves that they will be happier with that someone rather than be alone. Don't try to fit the other person into a mold you think you want or need due to the holes and fears in your life. If you do that, you're doing both of you a disservice. Love the skin you're in enough to stand tall, even if you do so alone. Try having a relationship with yourself before having a committed relationship with someone else. Make sure you love yourself enough to know when someone else doesn't love you. If your mate feels less than because you're more than, that mate is not your mate. Your significant other should encourage and compliment you, should treat you like the king/queen you are, and should be an enhancement to your life, not a jealous heavy or competitive hindrance. You should enable each other to be the best you can be and uplift, not tear each other down. When one rides high, the other should celebrate while awaiting their turn and should not undermine the other. There is no room for two when ego or selfishness is present in a relationship. Make sure your mate is your mate. You will know when you're with the "right" person. They'll help heal, not hurt, you. They will champion you, not judge you. They will love you unconditionally and only you. If you are with the right person and you are both complete within yourselves, you will be enough without question or evidence to the contrary. Don't change for anyone but you. The only real and lasting change can take place when you do it for yourself.

Whether it's losing family, a romantic interest, or some other trauma, loss is loss and the heartache and heartbreak from it is very real and telling of our heart condition. Some of us learn to bury hurt as a means to survive, but that is not the way to go. Don't shut out your feelings. It's what makes you human. While you can't choose what you feel, allowing yourself to feel is a better way. You must let it all back in so that you can let it out. Feel the pain, cry, hurt. Once you stop hurting, you can love again. Loss bring us face to face with the five traditional stages of grief— denial and isolation, anger, bargaining, depression, and acceptance. We deal with each of these in our own way, depending on where we are with our heart health. You may go through all or some of these stages and may even experience them in a different order. It is difficult at first, but how you come through the adversity depends on whether you choose to be destructive or constructive in responding. The only way to ensure constructive choices and behaviors is to have control over your emotions. That capability starts and ends with tuning into your channel on the journey of self-discovery to self-love, acceptance, and hope. You cannot simply flip a switch, nor would you want to. Life is meant to ebb and flow. You remove the ebb, life will not flow. Even though things don't make sense to our finite minds, faith and trust can give you peace. Our faith is made perfect in our trials and tribulations. Hold on to it to find willpower. Find your willpower, find your strength to love, lose, forgive, and live.

You cannot undo life, but you can choose to look forward and live. Choose now—past, present, or future? So many people wake up one day with a feeling that their life has passed them by, while living other people's dreams or spinning their wheels in circles of insanity with little to no fulfillment. Paralyzing regret, discontentment, worry, depression, and fear usually ensue followed by the thought, "How did I get here?!" The answer is, you lost you. That's how you got here. Good news! You can rediscover you. Where hope exists, there is life, and where life exists, there is hope. There's nothing to do about the past, the future is ahead, but the present is now and quite vacant. Tend to your present, or your future will pay the price. Your life may not be where you want it to be, but just start living one day at a time, one moment at a time, and appreciate every second. It's never too late for a fresh start and never too late to live in the now. However, take care not to just get in to fit in. We often seek comfort, identity, love, validation, and self-worth by socializing ourselves into scenes and behaviors that are unbecoming to us. Don't resign yourself to codependency that drain you, drag you down, or misdirect your path away from your purpose.

All of these situations are quick-fix drugs of choice, until you hit the wall. You will never find fulfillment or true happiness by these means. If you're not happy with yourself by yourself, you will never find happiness outside yourself, nor will you ever make someone else happy. Time decides whom you meet in your life, your heart decides whom you want in your life, and behavior decides who stays in your life. Make sure your heart is right for the right time. It will inform your behavior. When you let go of fear, pain, and feelings of inadequacy, you can finally be free to take on and conquer life. It all comes down to choices. Choose whether to win against life or to lose to yourself. Train your perspective to the wise disposition of one of my favorite recording artists, Joss Stone, concerning her experience in the ring of life, losing a round to love:

"Bruised but Not Broken" (Chorus)
And I'll be alright
And I'll love again
And the wounds will mend
I'm bruised but not broken
And the pain will fade
I'll get back on my feet
It's not the end of me
My heart is still open
I'm bruised but not broken

You may be bruised but you can avoid being broken. It's a mind thing; straighten yours out.

The timeless "Footprints" poem has been a refuge for me, and perhaps it can be for you too. Not only does it speak to the spiritual but also the physical. It reminds us that the spirit of God is ever present and carries us daily, particularly in difficult times. We tend to miss the earthly message here and the collateral beauty within due to the drudgery of life. Loved ones and special others come into our lives as surrogates to help carry us through emotional, physical, and spiritual voids until we can stand on our own, but they are not meant to fill them. When we are weak, they help us be strong. When we are fragmented, they help hold us together. When we are in the ring kicking life's butt, they cheer us on to help build our confidence. Recognize them for who they are and the role they were meant to play, but don't force them into your mold. They are God's assigned helpers to get you through periods when you cannot carry yourself or you need reassurance. If they were meant for a reason or a season, it suggests you're ready to stand on your own. Don't stunt their blessing or clip their wings by trying to hold on. When you love the skin you're in, you can spread love by letting go. If they were meant for a lifetime, you will know that, if you know yourself.

Stand up, brush yourself off, and adjust your crown. Loss and the conditions that come from it are temporary. God will restore you. While you work on you, focus on being light for those trapped in darkness; it will aid your perspective. Trust that your breakthrough is coming. You've got this. Have patience. The same hammer that shatters glass forges steel. Are you glass or are you steel? You choose. It truly is your choice, and it starts with your mind-set and approach to life. Strong is the NEW sexy! Develop your health and wellness from the inside out. Find and live the true you. Love the skin YOU'RE in!

Chapter 9

CONQUERING THE RING: FINDING PURPOSE

"Do not go where the path may lead, go instead where there is no path and leave a trail."

—Ralph Waldo Emerson

Dear Society,

With everyone busy trying to keep up with the Joneses or competing to whatever end, due to their conditioned state of mind, you have the opportunity, the gift, to carve out your niche. Be true to yourself. Awareness and knowledge are power and the road less traveled is exposure. Define your path and leave a trail. Be the one they didn't see coming!

One of the greatest human tragedies is unrealized potential. There is a reason your path does not look like another person's. It's called purpose. Too many people miss the off-ramp to their path because of distractions. They are busy looking left, right, or behind instead of straight ahead. There is a lesson here to be learned from horse racing. Racehorses wear blinders while on their racing path to prevent distractions, alleviate fear, and keep them looking forward, which provides an advantage by maintaining their focus on the race and what's ahead of them, not on the horses around them. It gives them the ability to manage their reality including existing and approaching distractions that might keep them from achieving their purpose and reaching their full potential. This small change in perspective of how a horse sees its surroundings encourages that horse to take chances it normally would not take. On some level, most of us fear our own greatness. We fear the responsibility that comes with meeting our full potential and walking in our true purpose. We settle for expected or "reasonable happiness" as a substitute for real happiness, leaving a hole of lack and incompleteness within us that festers in the soul. After all, who are we to want more and deserve more? Stop finding excuses to foil your dreams. Change your mind (make a decision), then change your mind-set and redirect to the positive.

Everything in life has a purpose, whether you can see it or not. If you have managed to overcome and find yourself in the ring on your way to conquering something, keep the intensity on. Don't allow outside forces to cause you to throw the fight. Don't make yourself smaller, to make others feel better. You were not meant to play small, and you certainly aren't responsible for the insecurity and jealousy of others. If you've worked hard for what you have accomplished, you have NO reason to apologize nor any need to justify your elevation. Your blessing is just that—YOURS. But know that your blessings were not given to you and your gifts were not made for you alone. Continue to maintain your work ethic and standards no matter what. Your performance will justify you and say all it needs to say. Discover what you are made of, break your chains, and be true to you. Reach back, teach, and uplift. "You are the difference maker." There's a reason you are where you are. Hint. You're there to learn, breathe life into, uplift others, or as a steppingstone to your elevation, which involves all of the above. It's yours to figure out and proceed accordingly. Whether you accept the assignment or not is your choice.

The Buddha once said, "Your purpose in life is to find your purpose and give your whole heart and soul to it." What you do is not who you are until you find your purpose. You will get insight into that person as you move through life and connect the dots; however, you will not truly understand nor live that life until you find your purpose. To do so, the metal must be ready for the Maker's hand; we are all uniquely and divinely made. Don't hide behind doing something good, when you're meant to do something great" (Brian Nieves, author of *The Dirty Dozen*). You may be scared, but channel that fear into strength. Affirm yourself. Tell yourself that you have the heart of a warrior . . . that you're brave, braver than anyone. Once you get off the wheel of insanity and break your chains, you can not only help yourself but also help others. It is time to face life. You can only conquer when you put "skin" in the game. If you want a test of faith, stamina, and training that will help you conquer life, then pursuing the path of an entrepreneur is the ultimate test.

I have found it to be true that most of us fear our own greatness and meeting our full potential. After musical performing artists, entrepreneurs are the next category of prolific divergent thinkers. You must be that kind of person. Your livelihood and survival depend on it. If by nature you are not a divergent thinker, this pursuit is a crash course in getting your mind right, tuning into your channel, accessing divergent ways of thinking and being, connecting the dots, and managing your reality. You will learn to stand on your own two feet and see the world differently. When pursuing entrepreneurial endeavors, you may be terrified on the inside, particularly if you are a first-generation entrepreneur (as I was), but fortitude will allow you to be a rock on the outside until you feel steady on the inside. What is fortitude? Fortitude is mental and emotional strength in facing difficulty, temptation, or adversity with courage. When you're in the ring with life, you will need it. Fortitude fuels better, quicker decision-making and clarity. There will be ups and downs, so expect them, take notes, and adjust to the opponent. Unbeknownst to me, this is what I had been training for.

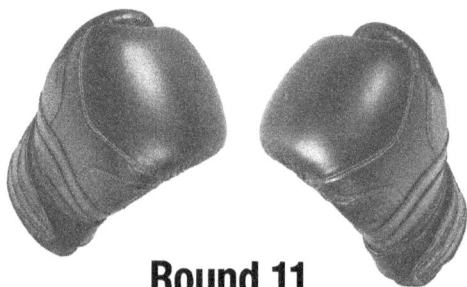

Round 11
Grown Up Stuff

While I had been curious as to my purpose, I had not been consciously seeking it. Something inside me always suppressed it for fear that it wasn't what I had planned; it wasn't what I had been studying for; it wasn't what others expected of me, given their knowledge of my gifts. I always knew it was bigger than me, but I thought that meant in one discipline and on an international concert stage. Even so, I always kept an open mind and followed the path I felt I was being led down. I did not start to see the formation of a bigger picture from connecting the dots until I took a HUGE leap of faith, left the university, and literally struck out on my own as an entrepreneur.

Leaving Indiana University was a new page in my book of life. After all, my world had revolved around it for fourteen years. Nevertheless, I was confident in my ability to move forward and conquer life. The mere fact that I was back in the ring on this level spoke volumes to me. I had been developing business concepts for some time before I decided to strike out, and they were all about improving the lives of others. So, I was comfortable with my prospects in that direction. I began to reflect on my passions and the times when I was truly happy. Those times were 1) onstage singing and touching hearts; 2) empowering minds and transforming lives; and 3) creating, improving or reconstructing entities for their betterment. It's only natural that I would start developing business concepts and models in these veins. The problem became that I did not manage my reality well. Talk about a bitter pill. I had a PhD in multitasking, literally and figuratively. However, it was that excellence in multitasking and "I am woman hear me roar" that worked against me. I came out swinging without a strategic plan for the fight, when I needed to approach the issue with deliberate caution and controlled confidence, planning, and conservation of energy, like a fox. Instead, my confidence drove my excitement, and full-on creative abandonment took me out of alignment with fiscal responsibilities and possibilities. I was creating business solutions for everything to change lives and the world all at one time! I knew better, but I didn't. I also did not take into full account my environment and other adversaries at the time. One thing led to another, and the next dots to connect took me to the Washington, DC, metro area.

It was ironic ... family and friends had been trying to get me to move to that area for at least ten years, but all things in their time. I was finally released from Bloomington, Indiana, after attending a Black Enterprise conference in Chicago, Illinois, in May of that year. Everyone I met was from the DC area, from the first people I met on the elevator, to those surrounding me in sessions and at banquet tables. I remember lying in bed the final night of the conference and contemplating where to go next. I knew in my spirit it was time to leave Indiana, but I was not sure where to go. For those of you who have experienced what I am about to share, you will get it. For those of you who have not, this may freak you out a bit (find your faith and you will get it). My heart and mind took me back to my homeland—Texas—yes, Texas is its own country to Texans, and the rest of the United States is its territory (you may be laughing but it is true). But as soon as I had that thought, I heard a voice clear as day say, "I told you Maryland." Even being a spiritual person and a woman of faith, this FREAKED ME OUT. Clearly, there was no one else in the room with me, and I was quite clear that I was sane . . . but I heard what I heard. My heart was racing, my mind was made up, and the next day I headed back home and began making arrangements for my move.

The preparation and process of the move happened so quickly that it was mind blowing and reassuring. I began the process at the end of May and the beginning of June, rented my house out in less than three weeks, and was driving to Maryland at the beginning of July. Transitioning was easy, but getting back on my feet was not. I networked, found a church home, and set out to re-establish my entrepreneurial endeavors in the Metro area. Things started to come together, but it was a hustle. The blows started coming incessantly, and life was seriously trying to conquer me. Luckily the bell rang and I retreated to my corner and my cornerman for guidance. An opportunity that would help me regroup and bring stability back into my life came across my e-mail one morning. The door opened so wide that I could not deny that it was for me. I didn't know how it would fit, but I did not worry about the outcome. What about my businesses? I continued operating my voice studio during the evenings but took a hiatus from my other independent pursuits. I knew I would eventually get back to them. I found myself on a foray back onto the job market, first working for a consulting firm for almost two years, then transitioning to service in the federal government. Honestly, I did question what the past several years had been about and reflected on the lessons learned: the central role of faith; the need for drive and focus; the importance of networking and developing relationships; consideration for scope of priority; strategic funding goals and calculated frugality; and above all, patience. I also learned a host of other lessons as well as realized to a full and applicable degree the importance of transferable skills and the capability to redefine yourself.

In the process of stepping back, I gained perspective. Taking the advice of my corner woman led me to conserve my energy as well as remember who I was and whose I was while the plan unfolded. It caused me to truthfully know the words of the old Gospel singer James Cleveland:

"I Don't Feel No Ways Tired" (Chorus)
I don't feel no ways tired
I've come too far from where I started from
Nobody told me that the road would be easy
I don't believe He brought me this far to leave me

Growing up with this song, I had no idea how real and powerful its words would be in my life. I've been sick, and I've been in trouble. I've been friendless, and I've been lonely, but God brought me. I DON'T believe He brought me this far to leave me. Neither should you. You see, I was not off-track, just on a different path that would converge with my purpose. I did not stay down. I kept getting back up to fight.

Just keep connecting the dots. Seemingly incongruent pieces of your life's puzzle will work together for your good, and divergent paths will converge if you view them through the right lens. Keep your eye on the prize of finding purpose, and you will do that. While you're at it, reconsider your worth, particularly you women. Society has assigned a lesser value to women, when we are actually worth more than the most precious jewels. Reprogram your mind. You are a queen. You are royalty. Live and act like it. Once you convince yourself, you will convince others and change your circumstances. Rule your space and respect yourself enough to believe in yourself. It's time to live your worth.

There is a biblical scripture, "Lean not to your own understanding." This perspective will help you move through life and give you a fighting chance. The closest you will come to "figuring out life" and why things happen the way they do is by finding your purpose. If you're going to conquer the ring, you must get out and stay out of your own head. It is easy to fall into traps in life and just float along, but if you are going to live a purpose-filled life, you will have to depart from the path of the "Joneses" and chart your own course. Don't worry about them and what they think.

Shine unapologetically! The very thing that makes you different, makes you special. It's your gift, your superpower, and the reason you were put on this earth. No one can fulfill it but you. Quiet your mind and silence the white noise of voices expressing opinions around you. Figure out what your purpose is, then follow your path wherever it may lead. Until you find it, you will always feel a void in your spirit that you cannot fill with anything but the right thing. The best way to quiet others' mouths and change their minds is to let your light shine.

The path I have walked has empowered me to be the diverse, strong, focused, loving, caring, and accomplished woman I am today. Was the journey perfect? The recovering perfectionist in me would say, "No." Nonetheless, it has been perfect to find my purpose without question. So many people live their life unfulfilled or discontent, settling on the position that it's just the way things are and must be. Yet when we approach life from that perspective, we live a self-fulfilling prophecy. It is not the way things have to be, whether they have always been that way or not. They are the way we choose to have them be through action or inaction. Wishing it to be so will do you no good. You must make it happen. Life may happen to you, but it will not happen for you without action and effort. When we consciously improve our circumstances, we can move mountains for not only ourselves but also others. Maya Angelou said, "All men are prepared to accomplish the incredible if their ideals are threatened." If your ideals to be happy and who you are without precondition or judgment are being threatened, do something about it. Once you've taken a long look at yourself and have worked on yourself, you will be ready to make a change. You will be a new person ready to find and walk in YOUR purpose. You cannot accomplish this if there is any doubt that you like the person staring back at you in the mirror.

In the documentary *Becoming Warren Buffett*, Buffet advises, "Look for the job you would take if you didn't need a job." This philosophy is guided by identifying your passions, which will get you closer to your purpose. Our passions are driven by our purpose. I am not talking about something you like to do to occupy your mind or space. Purpose comes from the essence of your being; that's why you must know who you are. Once you find your purpose, no one can stop you but you.

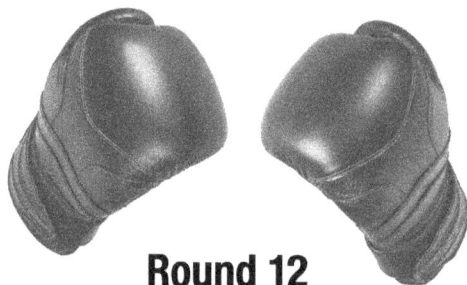

Round 12
(The Knockout)
Professional Confidence

I was introduced, or should I say reintroduced, to my purpose on a train ride leaving The Pentagon late one evening. It had come to me ten years earlier but I did not recognize it as such; I had not connected the dots. I stopped in the courtyard to take a prayer call, then went on to the Metro. I boarded the train and was standing near the doorway, when I heard a woman ask about the correct train to the Mt. Pleasant stop. The platform agent directed her to my train, to my car, and the doors immediately closed. As the train took off, I was sure of the destination I'd heard and questioned why that agent put her on the wrong train. I felt an urge to speak to her, to tell her that I thought she was on the wrong train and clarify where she was trying to go. She was shocked and said so. Most people do not speak on the DC Metro and do not concern themselves as to whether or not you are on the right train, even if they hear you are not. I was not the only one standing in that doorway who heard the exchange. After the woman got over her initial shock, I discovered she was a native Texan from my neck of the woods and presently lived in National Harbor, Maryland. She was an author heading to a seminar. This news hit me like a lightning bolt of déjà vu (feeling of familiarity) and déjà vécu (a feeling of recollection or having "already lived through" something). I felt an immediate conviction. I had been holding on to a list of book titles for at least ten years, but life kept preoccupying me and pushing it further and further away. I told her so, to which she responded, "I have a free ticket," and invited me to come (another moment of déjà vu related to the open window to Indiana University). Mind you, I was on my way to a concert at my church, National City Christian Church, in honor of the opening of the new Smithsonian African American Museum. I was so excited about this concert and was looking forward to connecting with old colleagues and friends. The word of this opportunity blocked everything out except that voice I heard back in Chicago telling me to go. I hesitated this time because of the commitment I had made to meet friends at the event. Meanwhile, the woman pulled out her book that had already been published as well as shared the evening's itinerary. That voice was stronger than ever, so I thanked her and decided to accompany her.

I thought I was going to a seminar for a few hours that evening. I had NO idea I would be attending a weekend-long boot camp with a publishing company that would transform my life and facilitate me to walk in my purpose. I had plans for the festivities that weekend! Funny thing about finding purpose. You will know it when you do. You will feel a great awakening, an adrenaline rush, motivation and commitment like never before; it's like finding the right companion for life (I'm told). As I sat there in the first five to ten minutes listening to the incomparable

Brian Nieves, I was in tears, crying uncontrollably and writing at the same time. This new book concept and title came to me that evening as well as the outline. That thing I had been wondering about, running from, then searching for, I had found it! Or did it help find me? When you take a leap of faith, the universe will move in your favor. You just jump, and I did. By the end of the weekend, the opportunity presented itself to sign with the company and become one of their authors. Publishing a book is a financial commitment, and I was not sure how I would make it happen. I almost walked away because of this concern, but I heard that now-familiar and clear voice telling me to share my story and step out on faith. So, I did, and you're reading this book because of it.

The woman who invited me did not return to the event. I never saw or heard from her again. As far as I am concerned, she was God's assigned and my purposeful angel. I realized that encounter was no accident, that it happened for a reason. That platform agent may or may not have known he was putting her on the wrong train. Nonetheless, it was essential to my personal journey. Our meeting led me to converging paths and finding purpose. The timely realization of my calling served to remind me that nothing happens by chance. Everything serves to guides our choices, actions, and instincts when we are in the ring with life. Acceptance of this fact, whether you like the reasons or not, is empowering and transformative particularly when you are in the ring. Changing how you look at life is a prerequisite for conquering it. Seek that which will bring you fulfillment and joy; tap into the voice of God for guidance. A healthy amount of fear in the process is natural. Just manage your reality and face the storms of life with fortitude. Fortitude will steady your emotions and calm the mind. Don't enter the ring without it. Fortitude is the source of your strength, focus, drive, and wisdom and is the complement to divergent thinking. When life goes for the jugular, fortitude will help you keep your composure to land the knockout punch. Face your storms in life with fortitude! Land that knockout punch by finding purpose.

Merton stated in his prologue, "Nothing at all makes sense, unless we admit, with John Donne, that: 'No man is an island, entire of itself; every man is a piece of the continent, a part of the main.'" When you have faith, and believe the best is yet to come, you will become a mountain mover for yourself and others (Pastor David Norris, CCFAN, Bloomington, IN). We cannot walk out our journey nor arrive at our purpose without life's involvement in circumstance, person, place, or thing. It's all connected and necessary. The great news is that you can choose how you respond. You can try running, but you can't hide from who you are or ignore your purpose if your desire is to conquer in the ring. Learn how to carve out your niche and become the integral part of life you were meant to be. You cannot do so by walking a path of convenience but only through deviating from the norm. Someone is waiting for you to love yourself enough to put skin in the game and show them the way. As Menjivar said, "The way that we can actually make a real difference . . . [is] by changing yourself . . . changing your own life and setting an example for the people around you and making a difference in your own community. But first you have to take care of yourself. If you don't take care of yourself, how can you possibly help anybody else?" The world needs difference makers. Be a change agent and use your power for good and not selfish reasons. Recall Quincy Roberts of Roberts Trucking in chapter 6? He is reaping the fruits of his divergent path and connecting life's dots and his community along with him. He took the first step in making a difference, and over a relatively short period of time, he learned and mastered his craft, finding his purpose. "Failure was not an option. I decided I was going to give it everything I had." He admitted, "I have not always been the confident man I am now. Confidence comes with experience . . . I have no regret. I really feel like I am living my life's purpose. There was a need there. I felt like I was the right person to tackle this need." That's the key. When you "feel" something that strongly in your core, and it's not driven by an emotional reaction predicated upon something else, that is your calling knocking. "I was completely unaware of my calling . . . it took others around me to bring it out," Roberts acknowledged in closing. He now employs over 250 people from his community (a reward in and of itself), and he is in a good space to excel and to share the love.

What is for you, is for you. A calling is a calling, and you will eventually answer it. Yes, people will ridicule, poke fun, try to convince you otherwise or try to frustrate your diverging path, intentionally or unintentionally. They may try to make you feel less than, but they are wrong. You are not a part of the problem but are the solution to life and living. The Apostle Paul wrote in Romans 8:

> [31]What, then, shall we say in response to these things? If God is for us, who can be against us? [33]Who will bring any charge against those whom God has chosen? It is God who justifies. [37]No, in all these things we are more than conquerors through him who loved us.

It takes a thick skin for a person to walk a divergent path. It also takes tremendous discipline to control the influence you have over others. If your purpose is leadership, you've chosen THE most difficult objective and to be in the public eye. You've chosen the way of influence, no matter the field or discipline. Accountability starts with you and extends outward. Your influence guides what others believe, how they act, and what they think. Influence bears responsibility. Control over it depends upon the messenger and the condition of your heart. Influence is power, and power has purpose, so guard against arrogance, which keeps you from understanding that you must be ready to assume and deal with power. Also, take care not to confuse power with privilege because there is a difference. The latter is bought with money, rank, and/or race. Are you disciplined enough to wield influence? If your mind-set is off, you are not ready for power. It's not about fighting to simply win or gain the appearance of respect. Power exists on a higher plane and is meant to affect, empower, and change the lives of others. How you use it also shapes your reality as a byproduct. As we are reminded in the *Divergent Series: Allegiant*, "Great leaders don't seek power. They are called by necessity." If your calling is to be a great leader, first, make sure you were called, and then you must reconcile with and live above your demons. Move in the purpose of power.

There's no such thing as perfect timing, only right timing. The right time for purpose to manifest in your life is after you've prepared and connected the dots. Take care not to force what is not for you. If it doesn't open, it's not your door. You may find the door was better closed. Wait for the open door. Once it does open, you will be ready; that's why you've been chosen. To whom much is given, much is required. Leaders set an example and make hard decisions in the best interest of the mission and their people, which requires them to be present, upfront, and impartial. Lead from the front, not from the side, the middle, or behind. Practice and master diplomacy; it is not people-pleasing, rather learning the art of tact. Check your biases, feelings, and constraining emotions at the door, but make sure to carry your conscious, ethics, and humanity with you.

Above all else, know your boundaries; without them, there's no reason to lead. There is no higher calling than service and sacrifice. The strength, courage, compassion, commitment, and dignity of mankind is never more apparent than when you undertake service. In whatever medium or by whatever means you serve, know that your work, even in silence, does not go unnoticed. Your calling is high and requires selflessness. God doesn't add another day to our lives because we need it. He gives them because someone out there needs you. Our purpose is bigger than we are and is never about us. The gift of choice allows us to live and choose for ourselves, but that is not our purpose. Your legacy and gift to the world concern others. Don't hide your light under a bushel! Become the servant leader you were put here to be. Recognition and awards will come, but the ones that truly count will come from a higher place. You will not be elevated by man but by your purpose and by walking in it. Your recognition will come because you love the skin you're in. It's nice to receive and give thanks; however, that is not your purpose.

What are you waiting for? Time may be favored for healing wounds and learning lessons, but it is not promised. Don't let time run out on you. Start living and find your purpose! You will know when you do, because it will be easy. If you've done all you can to prepare and survive the ring, start walking out your purpose. Even taking the smallest steps can eventually lead to you conquering the mountain. Sometimes the world spins too fast and you may have difficulty maintaining your center of gravity, if you've found it at all. But taking yourself out of the game is not the answer. Your mind is playing tricks on you. Instead, focus and shine your light on the dark forces trying to take you out. Their objective is to weaken and destroy you. They DO NOT want you to fulfill your purpose. If you're feeling powerless, take back your power.

Take control of your life and protect your mind, your armor, by whatever means necessary. Find your willpower to survive and thrive. Others are waiting to be liberated by your story. The right time will come. There's no perfect timing, only right timing. The right time will manifest after you've prepared and connected the dots. Tune into your channel, remain open and receptive in your thinking, continue to define your path, and manage your reality. You will arrive at your purpose. It's all a part of the journey of living. Anytime can be your time if it is the right time.

Do not make the fatal mistake of comparing yourself or judging your accomplishments against others. You are not in competition with anyone but yourself. You have no need to keep up with the Joneses or to fear failure. Failure is not an option, only a perception. You were created as a masterpiece by God, so act like it. Do not act arrogant, rude, condescending, or the like but rather confident, reassured, and grateful. Keep it fresh and don't sweat the small stuff. DO sweat missing out on your blessing because you decided not to step into the ring with life. Take your stance. Gloves up! Dance like your life depends upon it. It does! Learn to roll with and absorb the force of the jabs and punches life can throw; you will encounter wicked blows. No worries . . . just remember where and how the last one came. Expect the next and be prepared. Protect yourself and, most importantly, protect your mind. Any good boxer knows that if you drop your guard or let your opponent into your head, if it's not match over you're on your way. Fight the fight. The heart of a warrior is undeniable. Are you ready for the fight? The prize is an open door to conquering life. When it appears you're down for the count, get right back up with the mind-set "Surrender my hopes, dreams, who I am? What??? Not even an option." Conquer life one bout at a time, one bell at a time, until the final bell. Have the attitude of Muhammad Ali, "Float like a butterfly, sting like a bee. Hands can't touch what the eyes can't see." Be more than a conqueror. Always trust your heart and, most importantly, trust in your Higher Power. Tap into that unrelenting strength. You may be bloodied at given moments, but you will be unbowed. Respect the journey and appreciate the fight. It will ALL be worth it. May the truth of who you are set you free to find and walk in your purpose. Go get it! Get your blessing. Love the skin YOU'RE in!

Chapter 10

SURVIVING THE RING: THE JOURNEY OF LIVING

"If we did all the things we are capable of, we would astound ourselves."

—Thomas Edison

Dear Society,

Life is messy and imperfect because we are imperfect beings. Don't get caught up in decisions or worry about outcomes. If you've prepared and stepped into the ring with life, you are ready to conquer it. To do so, you must be willing to let go of conditioning and expectations. Enjoy the journey of living. Discover who you are and what you're made of. You may just surprise yourself.

One of the greatest ironies of life that I have discovered is that most people are not living, only existing. Social norms and conditioning have created haves and have-nots, social classes, and caste systems, shattering dreams and resigning those less fortunate to complacency and the acceptance of their circumstance. Within those structures lie an array of obstacles that must be overcome. What those subjected to these conditions have been challenged to realize is that "station" in life does not define who you are nor make you better than another person. It simply means one has known privilege over the other. Arriving at this perspective in a matter-of-fact way will not only liberate your thinking but also lead you down a path of discovery, recovery, dignity, and ownership of your past, present, and future. You are more than capable; however, the status quo does not want you to know that. When you find inner love, it will show you that and allow you to live your life with self-respect and respect for others. The path may be anything but normal and that's okay. You will be able to get back up every time you fall. Concern for measures that others take should not be your concern. YOUR definition of success and your measure are what matters. Concern yourself with defining your path where you are and with moving forward as well as with knowing what you stand for.

I have lived a colorful and forward-looking life. After connecting the dots and putting all the pieces together, I find myself healed, whole, and in a place where I have never felt stronger, reflecting upon the journey of living. One of the first rules of truly living that I learned along the way is to conquer fear by doing what you are most afraid of. It affirms your capability and strengthens your resolve. For some people, that means risking your heart to love again or for the first time. For others, it means even more. It's all according to your purpose. Life is a holistic experience. To miss any part of life is to walk the earth with holes in your armor. So, build your war chest with the tools that will help you conquer it and achieve your measure of success. Your divergence will allow you to walk among people and go places not everyone can. Champion your difference, your superpower. It will help you put it all together for the win, and the journey will lead you to your overall purpose.

We all begin training for life as children. We are who we are until the conditioning process starts to shape us through interactions. Our learning comes as we copy what others say and do. In the pursuit of mastering these behaviors, the competitive switch turns on and replaces our originality. After that, social constructs continually place us in the ring, pitting us against each other in the conquest for a given goal with rules of engagement that disparage original thinking and devalue individuality. Recognize this. Don't let this happen. We are more susceptible to this programming in our childhood. If we are teased about our physical appearance or a personality trait, we may become self-conscious and alter or hide our individuality. Boys tend to shut off their emotional side because "men aren't supposed to show emotion." Girls curtail their ambition because "it's a man's world." But as the late, great James Brown sang, "But it wouldn't be nothing, nothing without a woman or a girl." Belief systems form when we're young, and those beliefs continue to subconsciously run the show for the rest of our lives without us knowing it, until we bring them into consciousness. Who you were purposed to be has nothing to do with anyone else, so be mindful not to get caught up in competition or social expectations.

Your journey is not about who you should be according to others but rather about who you are. Why be a copy when you were born to be an original? Turn your switch back on and be the original you. Rediscover yourself by tuning into your channel. In other words, look inward and reprogram your mind. When you have strength of mind and purpose, the reactions from others that would otherwise adjust your course or how you revisit that same action in the future—conformity (informing you what you can't do, can't say, and how to act)—will not have power over you. You will be able to choose your path.

Meet life head-on with an inquisitive mind-set. "If you wish to see the truth, then hold no opinions for or against anything. To set up what you like against what you dislike is the disease of the mind" (Seng saying from *Hsin Hsin Ming*). Stated another way, "If you wish to see the truth, don't think for or against. Likes and dislikes are the mind's disease" (Zen master Hae Kwang). Be wary of socialized opinions. Seek truth for yourself. Conformity is the easy way out. Toeing the line or dancing a jig to someone else's tune, or opinion, is not living and will be a hindrance to defining your path. Living comes from an open heart and open mind. Opinions are not inherently bad, but opinionated minds can blind you to truth, as well as prohibit you from experiencing life. Opinions affect your choices and have consequences which reveal your state of mind and shine a light on your heart condition. Live life and base truth on merit, not words. While conformity may have its place in discipline, it has no place in finding your individuality or conquering life; you are not a mindless drone. Therefore, allowing the creative process to unfold in the childhood years is so important. If the foundation is laid and a child is trained to think outside the box, it will not be a foreign concept to the conscious or the subconscious as they move through life: 1) The pull toward conformity to conditioned norms will not affect their trajectory in the same way; 2) Their capacity for divergent thinking will be easier, if not natural; and 3) They will hold on to their individuality. Even if they choose to retreat for a time, they will re-emerge when it's time.

I am a realist. By social constructs, I was never set up to succeed in, much less conquer, life. But I have defied categorization. I began on the side of the underdog—a black female in America, born into a lower-income family, from the rural Deep South (yes, Texas is the South, and try telling a born-and-bred Texan otherwise). The "box" was not meant for me, so the experience of living inside or outside the box had its limits. The only option left was to live and think without a box. By doing so, I have come to realize that your station in life may give you a leg up, but it does not matter in the acquisition of character, drive, aptitude, or the discovery of the true you. With the right mind-set and the application of divergent thinking, you can turn your "underprivilege" into an asset. Do not allow yourself to succumb to despair or defeat. If you want something badly enough, you will step into the ring. Believe beyond a shadow of doubt that everything you've been through has brought you to where you are today—poised and ready to conquer life. You simply need to get out of your own way. If you are not where you want to be, continue to strive. We were blessed with free will, so make choices. Learn the lessons you are to learn from each situation. Should you lose a bout in the ring, learn and move on to the next bout. In the words of Marvel's Luke Cage, "Always forward, forward always!" Do the best you can at any given moment. The world IS unfair, and we were never promised it would be easy.

To manage your reality and change it, you must become aware. Sometimes it takes a bitter, hard pill to swallow and learn lessons you will not soon forget. Take your medicine, increase your knowledge, and internalize. Operate in the light and stay outside the shadows. Darkness cannot hide light, so live and stand for what is right. Speak up for yourself and others. Communicate your cares and concerns. Whatever your belief, or nonbelief, there is no denying that forces greater than us operate in and around us. There is a constant struggle between death and destruction, life and construction. They draw us into functional and dysfunctional interactions and relationships. We walk a fine line every day toward one or the other. Which way have you chosen to walk? It may account for your circumstances. Assess your daily interactions, activities, conversations, and circles; take inventory. Your decisions will either guide your path and breathe life into you or suffocate you. Life is difficult to do on your own, so seek life-giving friends and mentors for support. Asking for help is not a sign of weakness or a stigma; instead, it's a sign of strength and intelligence. Look for synergies in all aspects of life and take situations as they come. Conquering life comes down to the road not taken. That realization, my faith, and divergent thinking have been the great equalizers for me in my bouts.

If you feel heavy on your feet or stuck, try approaching life differently. Think differently. In an interview, the author of the manifesto *Say It Loud! I'm Black and I'm Proud? Really?*, K. Sylvester White, shared his recollection of words he heard for the first time in 1991 at the New Life Christian Center in San Antonio, Texas, from Dr. LaSalle R. Vaughn II: "If you always think what you always thought, you always get what you always got." When you see your way past the noise of thinking what you've always thought, you open yourself up for truth, healing, liberation, and empowerment. You have the chance to find and love the real you. Not everyone has to hit rock bottom to change course. According to White:

> To finally be happy; to finally be happy with yourself; to finally love yourself; to finally forge a new course in life, you've got to change how you think. In the African American community, if we are going to advance in this country, we've got to look at what we've been doing; we've got to look at who we've been depending on; we've got to look at what's been important to us; we've got to look at who we've been idolizing; and we've got to change all this thinking. If we want the country and the world to change their perspective about us, we've got to change how we think, which will change how we behave. But if we always think what we always thought, we're gonna continue to get, in this country, what we always got. We can look at that on a national scale and we can look at that on an individual scale.

He goes on to discuss divergent thinking in regard to personal development:

> Divergent thinking is changing what you always thought, thinking something new and doing things in a different way. Love yourself; learn how to love yourself; change your

134

ways. If you don't love yourself, something is wrong with your thinking. If you're not enjoying what you're doing, something's wrong with your thinking. If the world is a[n] abysmal place for you, something is wrong with your thinking. So, you got to change your thinking or you will keep getting more of the same.

Thought provoking words from K. Sylvester White. No matter who you are or where you come from, a shift in perspective and how you think can change your life. It can change how you see and relate to things and inform how you survive and thrive. That may mean lonely or uncomfortable situations at times, but the result will be the best you that you are supposed to be. So, if you think you'll never be more than what you presently are, think again.

Don't be afraid to redefine yourself and stay accountable to yourself. If you are not moving forward and changing, you are not living . . . you are not breathing. Don't just get in to fit in, and don't let others take you down a road you're not meant to go down. Think like yourself, act like yourself, and be who you were meant to be (no one else). You are unlike anyone else, so be proud of that fact but leave pride aside. Tune into your own channel and don't take on people's codependency. Even family, friends, associates, and colleagues have tremendous power over us, whether we or they realize it or not. Their influence and power of suggestion can work to our benefit or our harm. A simple concept and mantra to ingrain is program or be programmed. Let discernment be your guide and strength be your protection; remain vigilant. You are the only person responsible for your life's trajectory and successes. Don't expect anyone else to clear the way. Be accountable to and for yourself; maintain your integrity; keep healthy boundaries and your mind intact. Idle minds are easily caught unaware. Stay on track to your breakthrough. Remember, change your mind, change your mind-set. Start to conquer life one step at a time, one day at a time, one bout at a time until the final bell. Then claim your prize by finding purpose! Perhaps one of the most powerful stories of surviving, thriving, and overcoming shared with me during the interviews for this book was that of Dominique Leonard, writer and director of the stage play *Secret, Marriage & Vows* and founder of Dominique Leonard Entertainment. Dom and I knew each other in high school, but time and distance estranged us. I never would have imagined the path his life has taken. In high school, he was the proverbial All-American athlete in football, basketball, and track. He became a highly sought-after barber in the Houston area, cutting hair for the layman to the rich and famous as well as running party productions. Trying to "live large" and keep up with the Joneses got him caught up in situations, one of which led to his eight and a half years incarceration. Prior to going away, he also dabbled in writing. It was during his time in prison that he not only discovered his voice and calling, but also his individuality and who he was meant to be. Dominique says of his life, "The lessons I have learned have been hard but I never forgot where I came from and whose I was. My experiences have made me who I am and motivated me to lift up others." Life threw him a wicked blow that should've knocked him out like most, but he withstood the blow and fought back. Dominique chose to redefine himself and redirect his life path toward success in defiance of the odds and expectations.

At the entry of every door is the opportunity to choose a path. There are pathways we make and pathways we take. The combination is how you define your path. Just because it's there does not mean you have to take it. Allow for flexibility, spontaneity, adventure, and divergence along life's journey. Trying to follow a preplanned path that you, your parents, or elements of society have designed and analyzed to the detail can be restricting and limited. That method may work for a task, but it will not work in life. It will cause paralysis, and you will likely discover that path is not who you are or what you're about. Don't miss out on life-transforming opportunities and blessings because of rigid plans or expectations. Dare to be different; different is a privilege not a burden. Transcend factional thinking, and choose to take the detour instead of making the usual conditioned response. Do not run from the unexpected detours in life; rather, embrace them. They happen for a reason. Just choose your own way and not someone else's. There is no right or wrong, only knowledge gained, lessons learned, and progress on the journey of living. Society will tell you otherwise, instilling fear to protect its desired order for categorical uniformity that views divergence as a liability and discourages alternative paths, even though favor lies along those paths.

Preconditioning tells those who follow it that a Band-Aid is better than stitches even though the covered wound will leave a scar. It gives false comfort and reassures followers that the scar will fade over time, soothing lingering anxieties. Any means justifies the end in the quest for conditioned behavior (except divergence) because the trainers themselves are conditioned. They have not discovered their own individuality. Once you make that discovery, the value is priceless; you will not return to your previous condition. Think about factional thinking from a business and financial perspective. Does that thinking make sense to you? No question, for better or worse, business and money make the world go around. From an industry perspective, the goal of a business is to grow, develop, remain viable, and become profitable. In addition to diversifying holdings, businesses seek new ways of thinking and lead trends like employing individuals with not only needed skill sets but also healthy can-do attitudes and diverse experience. Divergence has proven to be an asset with practicing companies accomplishing their goals and leading their field. In the financial sector, the best advice given regarding building a retirement portfolio is to diversify it. If diversifying can be a good thing and an asset in business and finance, as well as other areas of life, why must it take on the role of liability in society, social models, and thinking? It doesn't!

Think back to chapter 1 and our discussion concerning the standard majority belief that anyone outside the norm is doing something wrong. In fact, they are doing everything right by choosing and defining their own path. If the inexhaustible list of divergents like Abraham Lincoln, Mother Teresa, John F. Kennedy, Maya Angelou, Mark Zuckerberg, Pope Francis, and Barack Obama had been unable to fly outside the norm, we would today be living a very different reality (perhaps the *Divergent Series* fictional reality). These people and others like them answered the call, stood apart, and conquered their fears to channel and exhibit fortitude in the face of persecutors and naysayers for the greater good. When you know, respect, and love who you are and dare to be different, you can start a chain reaction and even move mountains. Allowing anyone to keep you out of the ring for any reason is a loss for humanity. Historical acts and facts may have ushered in your "station" or situation in life, but you do not have to remain there. In the spirit of an admired friend and author Kristy Morrison, you have no choice but to *Make Life Happen*! Muster your will, put in the work, and conquer those obstacles that are trying to hold you down. There is no quick-fix formula to life. Adopt a divergent mind-set and just start living. Address the rest as you go. So many people live life unfulfilled or discontent and settle on the perspective that it's just the way things are. You are living a self-fulfilling prophecy. It is not the way things have to be. They are the way you choose to make them. Choose how you want to live and make the moves you need to make. Wishing it to be so will do you no good.

Without action and effort, you will always find yourself at the mercy of someone else's will. If you don't know how, ASK! Not everyone has had access or been exposed to essential life skills and experiences. There is no shame in that. Everyone has to start somewhere. Start building your toolkit for success with those who have the knowledge you need.

138

Brian South, founder of Choice Educational Consulting and author of *Demystifying College Admission: It's Your Choice*, helps students navigate their way through academics and in selecting the college of their choice, as well as helps parents both motivate students and strategize ways in which they can finance higher education. He partners with financial planners and insurance agents for solutions on how families can negotiate with college admissions officers and cut thousands of dollars in tuition without touching their retirement, immediate savings, or income. After working with clients who felt mystified about the college admissions process, Brian found that the lack of knowledge in how to study and prepare for the SAT or ACT, the right way to write an admissions essay, or even how to finance college, whether a low- or high-income family, affected the way the entire family felt about and perceived themselves as well as their ability to move forward and succeed in life. He believes the reason being is because some of the barriers to college admissions are outside of their control:

> The price of college, the way financial aid forms are set up, the standardized testing that they have to take, all of these things are artificially contrived, but they are ways in which students are measured on their merit for college admission. It's very difficult for students not to internalize the results they get, whether they are positive or negative, and form an opinion about themselves based on that criteria because it's so critical. For family members, they are putting so much effort into helping to get their child into college there's pressure on both ends. Some parents are working two and three jobs and put pressure on children to get exceptionally high grades, so that they have that competitive edge to get in.

On the other hand, children like me put the pressure on themselves because of what they live, hear, or observe in their environments. The pressure to be and do better is mental and self-inflicting performance anxiety. In an interview with Brian, he shared that he came from a highly dysfunctional and unsupportive family which was not supportive toward him getting an education. He left home at an early age and spent a number of years in New York City homeless. Even so, he carried a dream that he would one day get a college education and land a professional job. However, due to circumstances, he went an unconventional route, got a GED in his twenties, and then went through the community college system. From there he transferred to UC Berkeley and graduated. Brian experienced financial challenges along the way, as well as difficulty in finding people to support his dream. He had to dig deep and rely on his own resourcefulness to open doors. As a result of going through his life experiences and pain, he felt and found his calling in helping others who are struggling in their own unique ways through coaching, tutoring, and educational support toward their transition into college. See, Brian found a way to personally overcome the challenges and obstacles which presented themselves to him by embracing and loving the skin he was in. Instead of fleeing life, he fought and his experiences facilitated his recognition and ability to reach out to others, identify and empathize with their plight, and help them through their process given their circumstance. He has helped countless people find their voice and confidence, including special populations like foster care, non-traditional, current and formerly incarcerated students.

The lesson here for surviving the ring is that only an unwise person despises wisdom and instruction, clinging to their old ways. Seekers of wisdom in how to do and live are wise and recognize those with wisdom. Wisdom will teach you discipline, instructing you toward what is good and right. It will keep you away from pitfalls, teach you how to get out of negative situations, and light your path to success. Wisdom will help you grow and increase in knowledge, setting you ahead of the pace. It will impart discernment and insulate you from trickery. It facilitates understanding, teaches humility, and liberates your mind, body, and soul breathing life into all who have it. Those who ignore it waste their gifts and remain on the mat in the boxing ring of life, trapped by ropes in a circle of insanity, constantly fighting their own shadow. Are you wasting your gifts? Is it time for a pulse check? Be cognizant of your thoughts and assumptions. Sometimes we go off-track and need a reality check. Surround yourself with accountability partners, trusted individuals who will do that for you and not just those inclined to enable you because of their love connection to you. You need people around you who not only love you unconditionally but will also be real and tell you the truth no matter what. You can find plenty of people who will pump up your ego, but you need counters. Cheerleaders are meant to hype and cheer, while cornermen are meant to enlighten and teach. The latter will look out for your well-being and keep you from that fatal blow; know and understand the difference. You need a cornerman in your life. If you find yourself stagnant in your life or thinking, you are at a crossroads. That's the first clue. Change your ways! Change your thinking. Seek wisdom and the wise. It will make ALL the difference.

In addition to divergent thinking, you must have the personality traits and keys to gain access and conquer life. They include, but are not limited to, good judgment; a healthy amount of fear and understanding of a higher purpose; the drive and determination of an athlete; the creativity and finesse of an artist; and discipline, courage, confidence, strength, versatility, humility, dignity, follow through, and decisiveness. Think about the latter ... successful people spend little time sweating decisions. They make them quickly and often do not change their minds. People who are broke not only financially but also, and even more so, in mind and spirit make decisions slowly and change their minds often. Trust me . . . I have lived it. Get to a place where you believe your hype, even if the delivery takes longer. Confidence will come. Think of it as a muscle you must work daily. The exercising of this muscle will quiet the critical voice in your head which tells you that you can't do something and will bring forth the one which tells you that you can. Your ordinary actions will become extraordinary and inspire others. Always take the higher ground and go high, when others go low (Michelle Obama). Life forces us all to wear masks at times. The important thing is to recognize that fact and to take off the mask. Do not confuse the ability to transcend social and cultural boundaries with wearing a mask. They are not the same. In the latter, your identity and individuality are intact. In the former, not so much. Be who you are. It really is enough, and if it's not, consider the source. Seek your path and you will find it. Quiet your mind, learn to tune into your own channel, think divergently, connect the dots, and manage your reality. Success is marked according to personal scale and happiness. Decide what that is for you. You will reach YOUR measure of success and conquer life.

Take every experience for what it's worth, and while you're at it, reconsider YOUR worth. You are worth more than the most precious jewels, so live and act like it. Reprogram your mind. You are a queen. You are a king. Regardless of your circumstances, you are royalty. Once you convince yourself of this, you can convince others and change your circumstances. Control your thinking and redirect your thoughts away from anything otherwise. Rule your space and respect yourself enough to believe in yourself. It's time to live according to your worth. Conquer your mind. Just as an athlete trains the body, we must train our minds not only with knowledge but also speed, agility, strength, retention, and resourcefulness. Learn, grow, synthesize, and process, and then apply that knowledge and experience across other domains. Knowledge and skills are transferable, particularly when you think without a box. When your perspective changes, so will your capability. Progress over time. Once you've collected your toolkit, put on your tool belt; you're ready to define your path. How will you know when you have found success? When you can walk in freedom and purpose, and your presence alone speaks because of your inner peace. Teach others and liberate them. As Brian South would agree, the conditioned mind encourages us to remain safe and not take chances. It tells us things to keep us in a state of complacency. We all have to come to terms with our voices to achieve our own measure of greatness.

Conquer life by accepting yourself, your individuality, and your reason for being through divergent thinking and become invaluable in your personal and professional life. Change without loss or sacrifice is like peace without struggle; the world doesn't work that way. Don't let that fact distract you or hold you back. Diamonds take form with pressure. Perspective is everything. Perspective can be your best friend or your worst enemy. Overcome fear and enjoy the journey of living. Reconcile your past, accept your present, and walk in your future. Protect your mind and subject your thoughts to the positive. Life is a peculiar and worthy opponent. "The very nature of people is something to be overcome" (Steve Jobs). While musicians play their instruments, you conduct the orchestra. Lead from the front. It may be comfortable in the back, but no one can see you in the back. Your path will reveal itself to you when you're ready to see it. The journey of living, loving, and learning is so worth it, but it requires loving yourself first. Following societal norms for the sake of playing it safe is living beneath your worth. Shunning knowledge and choosing to remain in the same condition is not living. If you didn't already know, now you know that you have the power to choose. We make choices based on emotion, experience, and/or knowledge, which guide our action or inaction. Don't get caught up in the fear of living. Fear is power if you channel it right. Turn your fear into strength. Will you conquer life or will it conquer you? Don't worry about "normal." Remember, living is anything but normal. Colorful living opens the door and starts you down the road to empowerment. Meet life with courage and vigor. To conquer life, you must lead a purpose-driven life and that's anything but normal.

My life path has brought me in contact with famous, powerful, and privileged individuals around the world in every sector. The main lesson I have learned is that credentials are hollow and unimpressive without substance. Substance comes from knowledge of self and love. Your societal value or success is not determined by a piece of paper, by material things, or by how financially well-off you are. It is determined by looking at the thing you have that money can't buy—character. It's not what you do, it's about who you are. Standard operating procedures for societal norms and expectations may afford protocol respect to rank or title, but it does not make the man or woman. What you stand for and what you are about shape your identity and purpose. If you're merely placeholding to climb the ladder and check a box, you're selling yourself and others short. People spout notions of respect all the time without a clue as to how to get it. Respect cannot be bought, only earned through touching others' lives and hearts. If you don't respect yourself enough to check your behavior, others will not respect you. True respect is precious and hard won. Once you have it, keep it and it will help you maintain your self-respect. Respect comes upon you subtly when you're not trying, when you are about good and emanating light. You will know it when others admire and want to emulate you for things that have nothing to do with material gain. It is achieved by living and conquering your life fears, finding your purpose, and positively changing the lives of others. Monitor your communication and interactions. Don't say something permanently hurtful just because you're temporarily upset. Words matter and you cannot take them back; they can cause you to lose respect. Learning when to speak and when not to is a skill of discipline that will carry your far. In short, learn to control your feelings and passion. Take care not to shoot yourself in the foot. Don't be so high minded that you are no earthly good. To know and not do is to not know at all. You can be a part of the problem or part of the solution. You choose— problem or solution? The problem is that an unfortunate number of people choose "problem" based on their programming and the desire to belong. Consider how often you may witness or turn a blind eye to things that you know are wrong or, worse yet, support the wrongdoing of a "friend." Love yourself and that friend enough to be the corner wo/man. Every time you enable, consciously or subconsciously, you lose a piece of your humanity; kindness and benevolence are chipped away. Choose to sell out the problem, or continue hindering the solution and selling out yourself and others. Your humanity is calling. Find, unleash, and use your voice, your power for right, not might. Love the skin YOU'RE in!

PS

LOVE LETTER TO SOCIETY

Dear Society,

As I neared writing the end of this book, I found myself preoccupied with physical and emotional exhaustion, having concern over the publication date. I momentarily lost sight of my purpose for trying to reach the goal. Goals will come in time, when you are being led by in your purpose. Understand that they are not the same. Purpose fulfills and endures. Goals are rewarding but fleeting accomplishments. When you walk in your purpose, particularly for the greater good, forces will try to upset your assignment and cloud your judgment. Be ready and keep your gloves up. A good friend, prayer warrior, and Soror of Delta Sigma Theta Sorority reminded me of a few things concerning this—things I believe are invaluable to share with you (Thank you, Ebony Starke!):

God is still pouring into you what He wants you to write. Let him take care of the finish date. It will be launched at the perfect time and you'll look back and say it was not about you but all about Him. He is getting you ready for His purpose of the book and to elevate you! Do your part and He will do the rest. Everything happens for a reason. We make right turns, left turns, merges, U-turns, [go] straight and even backwards. We may be stopped by someone asking for directions (prayer or help). We may have to stop and ask for directions (prayer and help). I am learning that roads along the way will ultimately lead us to our destination despite dead ends, closed roads, and distractions in the way. We will still get to God's destination for our life. Just keep driving and know that distractions are intentional. It's all about His plan and what He wants for us. We don't want our plans. We want His because His are greater than what we can think or dream. WON'T HE DO IT?! YES, HE WILL!

We must choose our reality in this world and walk every step of it; lean on the everlasting arm that will give you strength to overcome all things (God). We are either victims or victors; I choose victor! I have come to realize that there is no time or reason for regret. Your every decision shapes you, and you choose whether to channel those experiences into negativity or positivity. Each of us in our own right is wonderfully made for our purpose, so stand tall no matter how long it takes or how difficult it may be.

My road has not been easy but life lessons learned invaluable. My journey has been all about preparing me for service and servant leadership, in the traditional and non-traditional sense. Moving, building, sparing, empowering, and liberating others and entities in thinking or circumstance has been my life work across diverse fields. In other words, borrowing a term from theology, my purpose is that of an intercessor between who/what they are now and who/what they were meant to be. In an interview with Engel Jones on the "Twelve Minute Convos" podcast, I was asked which of my talents was responsible for he and I meeting. The question caused a reel play of flashbacks in my mind and the answer came plain as day—influence. Throughout my life I have found myself in positions of influence, not from my own seeking, but out of necessity by simply connecting the dots. Some experiences challenging to accept at times, but nonetheless, required for my process of rediscovering, loving, and embracing my individuality and calling. Now that I am older and wiser, I can truly say that all has worked together for my good. Every tear, pain, and emotion has been worth it. I walk in humble confidence every day knowing that I am anything but normal and was meant to be that way. Now, when I step into the ring with life, I am unconquerable because I know I am the value-add, even if my opponent for the day doesn't know it. It's not about who or what you face. It's about getting your mind right to face anything and love who you are, when and where you are. Learn this and you will be ready to face any obstacle. Once you change your attitude, hone your skill sets, and know what you can offer, every match lends perspective; it's not as difficult as you may think. YOU are the value-add. Keep repeating it until you believe it and it will be true.

Living is transformative and the purpose of life itself. It brings a re-evaluation of thought, reassessment of values, and identifies purpose. The process of living itself tests clarity of knowledge or lack thereof. Even surrounding this book project, I found transformation in writing. A book is a living, breathing entity of its own and it takes on a life of its own. Sometimes the project you thought you were starting may not necessarily be the one you end up with; it also changes and grows. So, be open for redefinition in your life. It's fine to have a basic concept but be flexible. As Miguel Ruiz reminds us in The Four Agreements and The Fifth Agreement, be impeccable with your word, don't make assumptions, do not take anything personally, and always do your best. His premise is that we make a lot of conscious and subconscious agreements with ourselves and others that are simply contrived human lies and artifacts. Understand why they exist (to make others feel better about themselves) and do not internalize them. Here are a few tips that I have lived by to boost my confidence, avert meltdowns, believe in myself, and be my own cheerleader in the goal of conquering life:

- Work is work. Perform to your best ability and do it with excellence but understand it is not life or death. If you're fortunate, you will find work in the area you are purposed for, which will immediately boost your confidence and prevent meltdowns.
- Change your mind and mind-set about the unfamiliar and about new beginnings. Accept and embrace change as an opportunity.
- Find out who you are. Set yourself on the path to self-love: tune into your channel, explore and discover your individuality, reconcile issues, and grow.
- Think divergently. Master the concept for presence of mind as well as immediate and absolute recall for the highest and best performance in all endeavors, personally and professionally.
- Understand that competition is in your mind. You and you alone have the power to regulate it.
- Give yourself a break from expectations and perfectionism. They can lead to performance anxiety and ultimately lead to disappointment.
- Identify colleagues and mentors who are willing and able to help you through your career and life journey with no expectations.
- Have faith. Reaffirm yourself daily and do not worry about seeking approval or accolades; they will come.
- Do not be afraid to redefine yourself if the fit isn't a good one. There's nothing wrong with changing course. Just keep connecting the dots and you will find your way.

- Above all, your health and sanity are the highest priority. If they are not well, you are not well. Conquering life then becomes irrelevant.

On this journey of living, if you are going to connect the dots, walk in purpose, and find fulfillment, you must be led by your heart and the truth of who we are—strong, intelligent, diverse, adaptable, wise, and tried by fire. Believe this and internalize it. You were meant to do and be more. You were meant to be different. You are the apple of God's eye. Look inward and truly see yourself. You are stronger than you could ever imagine. There's a reason people gravitate to you and want to hear what you say. You are extraordinary and your individuality is waiting for rebirth. You know what to do . . . change your mind and mind-set. The process will not look pretty and certainly will not be perfect, but you are more than a conqueror. Don't mind those who mock or reject you. Exceptional things are rejected all the time by people who can't afford them. Even Jesus was mocked and rejected by people who could not/would not understand Him or His purpose. Consider yourself in great company and count it all joy. You have been set apart for a reason, a purpose. There is a reason you don't fit in. You are not the norm but the exception. You are priceless! Everyone can't afford you. Always remember the example of a diamond. It may be hidden and covered by dirt for a time, but then it is uncovered, pressured, polished, and made to shine. So, shine unapologetically outside the norm!

If you are a divergent soul or have that spirit, step into your role and learn how to carve out your niche. The world needs difference makers, so be a change agent. As Cris Houston reminded me, "The higher the calling, the higher the heat." You have the resilience to stand when it counts and when called higher. You are multifaceted in your construction, makeup, gifts, talents, and thinking for a reason. Your decisions will be more difficult; your path bumpier than the norm; your morals, ethics, ways of thinking, and beliefs tested. You are not being punished but prepared. Be reassured that life is not a popularity contest, a competition among different circles, or solely a means to an end. It's about finding truth and fulfillment within, accepting it, then allowing that confidence to radiate out and change everything and everyone around you for the better. Small minds will not prevent you from doing something; they are merely obstacles to climb over. Those individuals who are stuck in their ways choose to remain so and are not your concern, but rather only those who have an ear to hear with an open mind and heart.

Face the storms of life with fortitude; it will all come together. In this instant gratifying, fast paced, information age world, things just don't seem to come soon enough. We want things yesterday, and in reality, yesterday is tomorrow or the next day or sometime in the future. Like a plant, know and be confident that you will grow and germinate in the right season. Stay prayerful; prayer truly changes things. Meanwhile, work to become love in all that you do and think. Love is the heartbeat of the world, and without it, we are lost. To become love requires extraordinary openness and beauty of mind, spirit, heart; beauty doesn't just dwell in the senses. Walking in love does not mean you are perfect, without spot or blemish; you will falter at times. It simply means you've worked hard on yourself to understand and appreciate you for you. Once you do that, you can love and receive love from others and appreciate the worth of every individual. It's not an easy thing because it requires you to face and reconcile your demons and conditioned beliefs. But to get to the other side of true love, it is a requirement. There will be those who try to subjugate you, but they cannot do that when love and purpose are your guides. Be encouraged to walk out your path with a generous heart and spirit, no matter your situation. It will maintain your heart health and will not return to you void. Whether in acts of time, spirit, monetary, or otherwise, your generosity will make room for you. Its return may appear questionable or even elusive to your human mind, but it will return and eventually make sense. Triumphant or challenged, make every day that you draw breath a thanksgiving because your way is prepared. Just start living and have faith. Look in the mirror every day and love what you see. It is not an act of arrogance, particularly if it comes from a place of appreciation for the struggles you've overcome and the progress you've made. Self-assessment, hard work, and transformation SHOULD yield such a response. If it doesn't, you've not done it right. Try again. If you don't like something, complaining and complacency will give no result. Figure out how to make it better.

Do not concern yourself with acceptance from others or buy-into their artificial standards; human beings are fickle. People who are judgmental will always be judgmental until enlightened; most of them do not have enough self-awareness to even know why they say the things they say. Perspective is everything and finite thinking can only see so much when perspective is limited to that socialized reality. When you listen to opinions or feedback, measure it and decide whether it applies to you or not; it may just be what Brian South likes to call a "data dump." Question everything that seems contrary to the essence of your core being. Do not make entire life changes based on assumption, and in the process of living your life, do not allow the cares of this world to destroy or devastate you, especially to the point of wanting to take yourself out of it. You have the power to decide that you want to raise your standards or change who you are, or that actually you are happy where and with who you are. Put off debilitating conditioning toward social norms and expectations and program yourself into the right frame of mind for the right people to notice, and they will notice;

trust me. Favor isn't fair. Have the audacity and fearlessness to proclaim your individuality and favor will come to you. Strong is the new sexy! Don't trend, make the trend. Join the movement, tell your story, and start defining paths. Spread the empowering message of loving and living from the inside out!

With love because of the skin I'm in,

Doc

www.ingramcontent.com/pod-product-compliance
Lightning Source LLC
Chambersburg PA
CBHW021233090426
42740CB00006B/514